THIMBLEBERRIES®

Learning to Quilt

with

by Lynette Jensen

Landauer Books

THIMBLEBERRIES®
Learning to Quilt
with
Jiffy Quilts™

This book was designed, produced, and published by Landauer Books
A division of Landauer Corporation
3100 NW 101st Street, Urbandale, Iowa 50322
www.landauercorp.com 800/557-2144

President: Jeramy Lanigan Landauer
Director of Sales & Operations: Kitty Jacobson
Editor-in-Chief: Becky Johnston
Managing Editor: Jeri Simon
Art Director: Laurel Albright
Creative Director: Lynette Jensen
Photographer: Craig Anderson
Photostyling: Lynette Jensen
Technical Writer: Sue Bahr
Contributing Technical Writer: Rhonda Matus
Technical Illustrator: Lisa Kirchoff

We also wish to thank the support staff of the Thimbleberries® Design Studio:
Sherry Husske, Virginia Brodd, Renae Ashwill, Ardelle Paulson, Julie Jergens, Clarine Howe,
Tracy Schrantz, Amy Albrecht, and Leone Rusch.

The following manufacturers are licensed to sell Thimbleberries® products:
Thimbleberries® Rugs (www.colonialmills.com);
Thimbleberries® Quilt Stencils (www.quiltingcreations.com);
Thimbleberries® Sewing Thread (www.robison-anton.com); and
Thimbleberries® Fabrics (RJR Fabrics available at independent quilt shops).

Printed in China 10 9 8 7 6 5 4 3 2 1

Library of Congress Cataloging-in-Publication Data
available on request.

ISBN 10: 1-890621-51-X

ISBN 13: 978-1-890621-51-3

contents

Learning to Quilt is Fun

Since most of the Thimbleberries® staff are ardent quilters, it is only natural that their enthusiasm for quilting rubs off on the younger generation. Here and on the cover, Kristen Kirchoff, a high school senior and daughter of Lisa, our technical illustrator, practices basic techniques you'll find featured in the pages of this book.

introduction

After falling in love with antique quilts I decided to make my own. I love the color and geometry of quilts and what they represent—comfort, home and family. After learning how to quilt, one thing led to another and soon I was teaching the art of quiltmaking, which ultimately led to designing quilt patterns and fabrics since the coordination of prints, colors and quilt patterns created a distinctive look.

I discovered that by designing my own line of coordinating prints, solids and plaids, I could get exactly what I needed for my growing collection of pieced patchwork. Today, Thimbleberries® fabrics are featured in more than 2500 independent quilt shops and nearly 1000 of these shops host a Thimbleberries® Quilt Club that meets regularly.

One of the reasons that Thimbleberries® has been so well-received is that I make it easy for quilters to enjoy the wonderful heritage craft of quiltmaking. In today's busy world, time is limited. I show quilters what to do with the fabrics without spending a lifetime creating a quilt. In 30 years of teaching, I've also developed a system of quiltmaking that uses clear and simple instructions to help even first-time quilters build confidence and skills.

Begin by reading the instructions on the following pages thoroughly. When you're finished, choose a Jiffy Quilt or runner that suits your style. You'll find quilting guides offered for several of the projects for use in hand or machine quilting.

But most of all, throughout the creative and soul-satisfying process of learning to quilt—enjoy!

My Best,

Lynette Jensen

basic parts of a quilt

Quilting is quite simply

securing three layers of cloth that have been sandwiched together with simple stitches called quilting.

A TOP LAYER (the quilt top) is made up of individually shaped pieces of cloth joined or "pieced" into a geometric or random design by hand or machine sewing.

A FILLER LAYER (usually batting) creates the raised effect on the quilt surface when it is compressed by ties or stitching.

A BOTTOM LAYER (the backing) can be a whole piece of cloth or several fabrics joined together.

Quilting has a language of its own, but becoming familiar with a few terms will take you from start to finish on your first quilt. The diagram below and on the opposite page shows basic terms that will be referred to in the pages that follow. You'll find brief definitions of these and other frequently used terms in the Glossary on page 142.

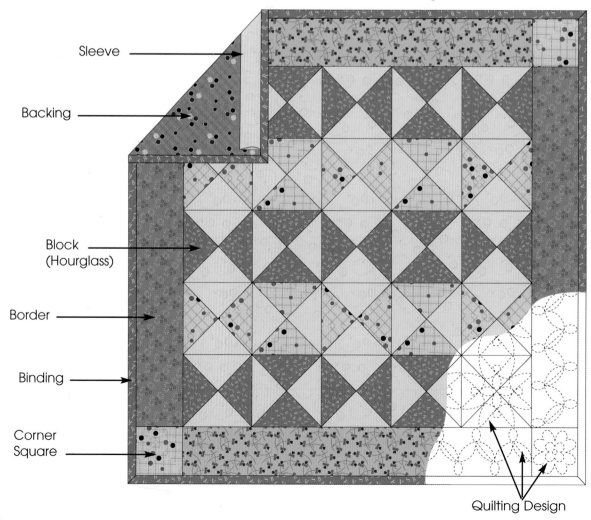

Sleeve

Backing

Block (Hourglass)

Border

Binding

Corner Square

Quilting Design

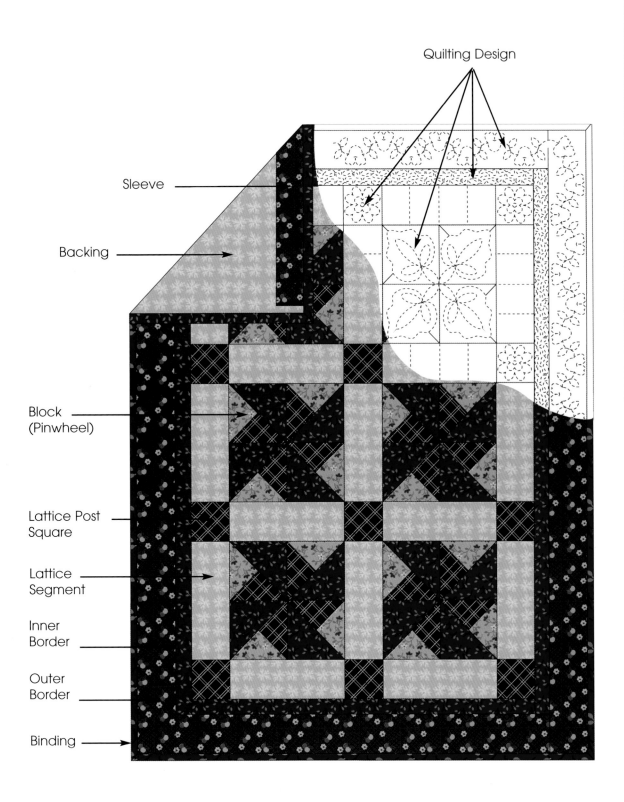

Quilting Design

Sleeve

Backing

Block
(Pinwheel)

Lattice Post
Square

Lattice
Segment

Inner
Border

Outer
Border

Binding

GATHERING

Equipment, Tools & Supplies

Discover how easy it is to get started in quilting with an illustrated guide to the simple tools and supplies you need to have on hand. As a beginner you can make beautiful quilts with a modest investment in a sewing machine.

On the following pages you'll find that my list of favorites is short and sweet. I find myself using the same basic equipment, tools and supplies again and again, year after year, because they are always accurate and dependable.

☑ *sewing machine*

☑ *needles*

☑ *silk pins*

☑ *magnetic pincushion*

☑ *thread*

☑ *seam ripper*

Needles

For piecing fabrics together on your sewing machine, use a size 70/10 or 80/12 sharp sewing machine needle or an 80/12 universal needle. Note that the sewing machine needles are available in European and U.S. sizes. As an example, for the sewing machine needle recommended above, the larger number (70) is European; the smaller number (10) is U.S.

For machine quilting, change the sewing machine needle from the one used for assembling the quilt top to one that's thicker and stronger for quilting through the three sandwich layers. A size 75/11 quilting needle or a size 80/12 jeans needle is recommended.

Sewing Machine

For beginning quiltmaking, you'll need two basic pieces of equipment—a sewing machine and an iron. Whether or not you invest in a machine with all the "bells and whistles," just make sure the machine you use sews an accurate straight stitch. Then, read the manual and review the machine's features. Make a practice of routine cleaning and take the machine to a professional for regular check-ups.

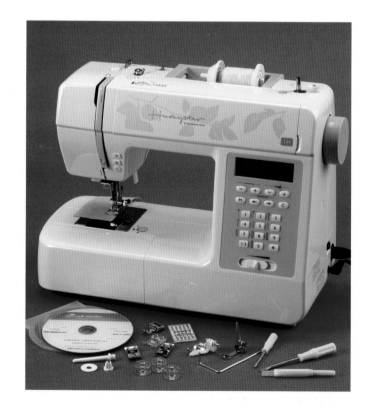

Silk Pins

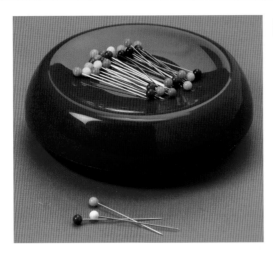

I've found that the Grabbit® magnetic pincushion has a surface that is large enough to hold a good supply of straight pins and a magnet strong enough to keep them securely in place.

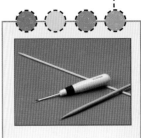

TIP:

It's helpful to have a tool for reworking or feeding fabric under the presser foot, especially when you're working on a project which requires long sewn strips. The handiest aid is a seam ripper. A bamboo skewer or a stiletto also serve as helpful fabric guides.

Because silk pins are long and thin they are less likely to leave large holes in your fabric. Silk pins also increase accuracy in pinning pieces or blocks together and are easily pressed over as well.

Choosing Thread Weight

Choose a 50- or 60-weight two- or three-ply 100 percent cotton thread for your sewing machine—threaded through the needle and wound in the bobbin.

To complement the Thimbleberries® color palette, I've designed a coordinated seasonal color collection of 100 percent Egyptian Cotton Mini-King Spools of sewing thread.

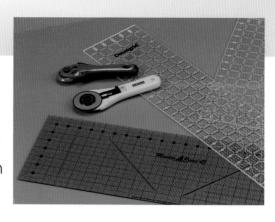

- ☑ *scissors*
- ☑ *cutting mat*
- ☑ *acrylic rulers*
- ☑ *rotary cutter*
- ☑ *iron*
- ☑ *pressing surface*

Rotary Cutting

A self-healing rotary cutting mat, clear acrylic rulers with 1/8-inch markings and a rotary cutter are necessary tools for accurate cutting.

A 24 x 36-inch wide self-healing mat easily accommodates most fabrics. I find the lines are fine and accurate on the 24 x 36-inch Olfa® rotary cutting mat and they stay visible longer than on others.

The clear acrylic ruler you purchase should measure at least 6 x 24-inches and be easy to read—the larger size will prove invaluable to long-term quiltmaking success. To me, a long acrylic ruler is indispensable for accurate rotary cutting. I prefer the Omnigrid® 6 x 24-inch grid acrylic ruler for cutting long strips and for squaring up fabrics and quilt tops and the Master Piece® 45-degree (8 x 24-inch) acrylic ruler for cutting 6- to 8-inch wide borders. I sometimes tape together two 6 x 24-inch acrylic rulers for ease in cutting borders up to 12-inches wide.

The 15-inch Omnigrid® square acrylic ruler is great for squaring up individual blocks and corners of a quilt top, for cutting strips up to 15-inches wide or long, and for trimming side and corner triangles of fabric.

The Olfa® rotary cutter with the 2-1/2-inch blade cuts easily through many layers of fabric. The Dritz™ rotary cutter offers a unique safety lock feature.

Pressing

Pressing is an important step in quiltmaking. As a general rule, you should never cross a stitched seam with another seam unless it has been pressed. Therefore, every time you stitch a seam, it needs to be pressed before adding another piece. Quite often it seems as if you press as much as you sew.

Most quilters find the moisture in steam helps. Steam will not distort the shapes as long as the pressing motion is used.

It is important that you press rather than iron the seams. Unlike ironing, pressing is a firm, up-and-down motion that will flatten the seams but not distort the piecing.

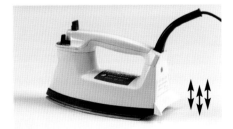

The back-and-forth motion of ironing will stretch and distort small pieces of fabric. A tried-but-true rule is to press seam allowances in one direction, toward the darker fabric. Often, background fabrics are light in color and pressing toward the darker fabric prevents the seam allowances from showing through to the right side.

NOTE: *For ease in hand quilting, the quilting lines should fall on the side of the seam which is opposite to the seam allowance. Occasionally seams need to be pressed in the opposite direction so the seams of different units will fit together more easily, often referred to as "nesting" seams.*

When sewing together two units with opposing seam allowances, use a seam ripper tip to gently guide the units under the presser foot. At times it may be necessary to press the seams again to make the units fit better.

Always try to achieve the least bulk in any one area. Regardless of which direction you press seams, there will always be a little bulk.

TIP:

For pressing individual pieces, blocks and quilt tops, I use an 18 x 48-inch sheet of plywood covered with several layers of cotton fiberfill and topped with a layer of muslin stapled to the back. The 48-inch length allows me to press an entire width of fabric at one time without the need to reposition it. The square ends are better than tapered ends on an ironing board for pressing finished quilt tops.

CHOOSING

Fabric Print, Color & Value

Shopping for fabric is fun when you know exactly what
fabrics to choose for your first quilt. All you need to
keep in mind are a few of the basic rules of fabric print,
color and value described on the next few pages.

You'll also find it helpful when choosing fabric to know
how to shop for quality and quantity as well as
identify the bias and the grain of fabric. After you've
purchased fabric to add to your stash at home, it's best to
test your fabric for both shrinkage and colorfastness.

Choosing Fabric Prints

Cozy country scrap quilts have heavily influenced my preferences in fabric design. I enjoy the challenge of blending a large number of fabrics into a pleasing collection featuring the following elements:

- SUBTLE SOLIDS are tone-on-tone color combinations with subtle, allover random prints treated as a solid color in a quilt.

- SMALL BLENDER PRINTS offer color, design and texture without a lot of differences in color values.

- LARGE-SCALE PRINTS are best used effectively as outside borders and large patches and alternating, unpieced blocks—usually no more than one per quilt.

- WOVEN PLAIDS & CHECKS or PRINTED GEOMETRICS add a bit of geometry and a rest for the eye between the Small Blenders and the Large-Scale Prints. They should be used sparingly because the bold images or strong color definition can sometimes interfere with and distract from the pieced design.

NOTE: *The fabrics shown here may or may not be currently available. However, the unique feature of Thimbleberries® is that the fabrics can easily be mixed and matched because they blend from group to group.*

Subtle Solids

Small Blender Prints

Large-Scale Prints

Woven Plaids & Checks   *Printed* Geometrics

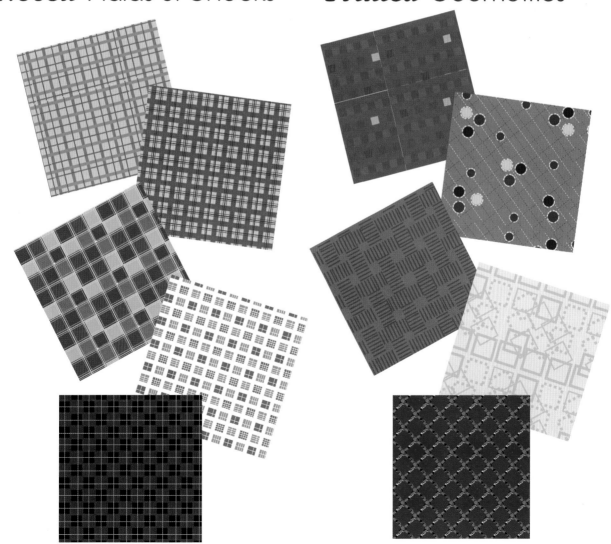

Choosing Color

Fabric color is a reflection of your personal preferences in decorating. When designing quilts for Thimbleberries®, I gather fabrics in a palette of colors that blend perfectly for each season to transition through the year in style.

When choosing fabrics for your quilt, you may want to be inspired by the colors of nature that have stood the test of time—from the golden sunshine to blue sky and green grass. Warm colors are in shades of yellow, orange and red. Cool colors are in shades of blue, green and purple. Most colors can be described as warm or cool as shown in the range below.

warm

cool

Establishing Value

Value is the lightness or darkness of a color. Value describes color as it appears in a black and white photograph. As you make your fabric selections, you'll see that their values are relative to each other, depending on how they are placed in a quilt.

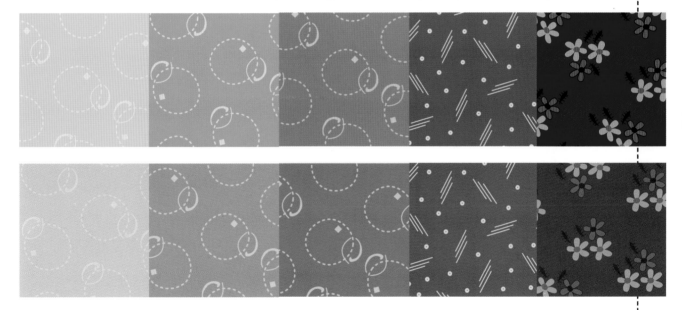

light   dark

Choosing Fabric

Yardage for the Jiffy Quilts by Thimbleberries® is based on 42-inch-wide fabric. The width of the fabric you purchase will determine the number of strips you need to cut and, of course, affect the amount of fabric you have left over. Generally, the yardage given in Thimbleberries® patterns is generous enough that you can confidently cut your pattern pieces.

The best fabric for quiltmaking is 100 percent cotton. It's easy to cut, easy to sew, and holds up well to handling. If possible, avoid all polyester fabrics and polyester-cotton blend fabrics because polyester tends to pill and can be stretchy.

Shopping for Fabric

Fabric usually comes from the mill in long lengths folded in half and wrapped around a cardboard core. The finished product is called a bolt from which fabric is unwrapped and is almost always sold in 1/4-, 1/3-, 1/2- or 1-yard lengths. Information about the fabric is printed on the label at the end of the cardboard core. It is here that you'll find the key ingredient: 100 percent cotton.

Not all 100 percent cotton cloth (or fabric) sold in stores is created equally. Though a fabric pattern may appear the same, the milling process for creating the woven goods onto which a design is printed may differ—which will be reflected in the price per yard. I always recommend choosing higher quality fabrics for a quilt. It will hold its color and strength through many years of use.

Beginning with Fat Quarters

One of the quilting terms you'll hear most often is fat quarter or fat fourth. What is a fat quarter? It's an approximately 18 x 20-inch piece of fabric that has been cut from a yard of fabric. Four fat quarters can be cut from 1-yard of fabric.

By making a small investment in pieces of fabric such as fat quarters, you can try out various combinations of prints. After you've experimented and gained confidence in your fabric selections, you can invest in larger quantities of fabric purchased by the yard.

Using Grain

The fabric you purchase still has selvage and before beginning to handle or cut your fabric, it's helpful to be able to recognize and understand its basic characteristics. Fabric is produced in the mill with identifiable grain or direction. These are: lengthwise, crosswise and bias.

The lengthwise grain is the direction that fabric comes off the milling machine, and is parallel to the selvage. This grain of the fabric has the least stretch and the greatest strength.

The crosswise grain is the short distance that spans a bolt's 42-inch to 44-inch width. The crosswise grain, or width of grain, is between two sides called selvages. This grain of the fabric has medium stretch and medium strength.

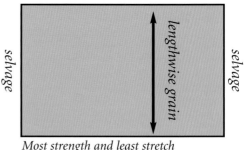

Most strength and least stretch

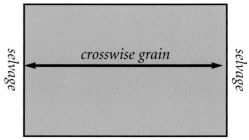

Medium strength and medium stretch

Avoiding Bias

The 45-degree angle on a piece of fabric is the bias and the direction with the most stretch. I suggest avoiding sewing on the bias until you're confident handling fabric. With practice and careful handling, bias edges can be sewn and are best for making curves.

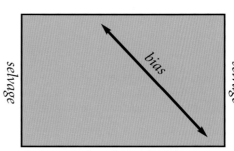

Least strength and most stretch

Prewashing

Prewashing and pressing fabrics helps test for colorfastness and possible shrinkage. If you choose to prewash, wash in cool water and dry in a cool to moderate dryer. Industry standards suggest that line drying is best. Shrinkage is generally very minimal and not often a concern.

A good way to test your fabric for both shrinkage and colorfastness is to cut a 3-inch square of fabric. Soak the fabric in a bowl filled with water. Squeeze the water out of the fabric and press it dry on a piece of muslin. If the fabric is going to release color, it will do so either in the water or when it is pressed dry. Remeasure the 3-inch fabric square, and if it has changed in size more than 1/4-inch then wash, dry and press the entire yardage. This little test could save you hours in prewashing and pressing.

Flannel and other loosely woven fabrics almost always have shrinkage and will need prewashing and drying.

Fabric that HAS NOT been prewashed...	Fabric that HAS been prewashed...
requires less handling. You can start cutting and sewing it immediately.	is less likely to bleed when the quilt is eventually washed. Washing away the excess dye helps set the colors and can save future headaches. (Imagine discovering upon washing a finished quilt that the fabric has permanently bled onto other fabrics.) Colors most likely to bleed are red and dark blue.
is used on the front and back of a quilt and will shrink at the same rate (2% to 3%) when a finished quilt is washed. This results in a quilt with an attractive puffiness around quilting—a look and characteristic that many quilters desire.	is now preshrunk (2% to 3% shrink rate), providing assurance that when it's time to wash a quilt, the quilt will not shrink further or unevenly.
handles well. The crispness and body of a new fabric can make cutting and piecing easier.	has had any surface finish or stiffness washed from its fibers, making it easier to quilt. Quilters who like the crispness and body of new fabric because it's easier to work with, restore it after washing by spraying the fabric with sizing or starch while pressing.

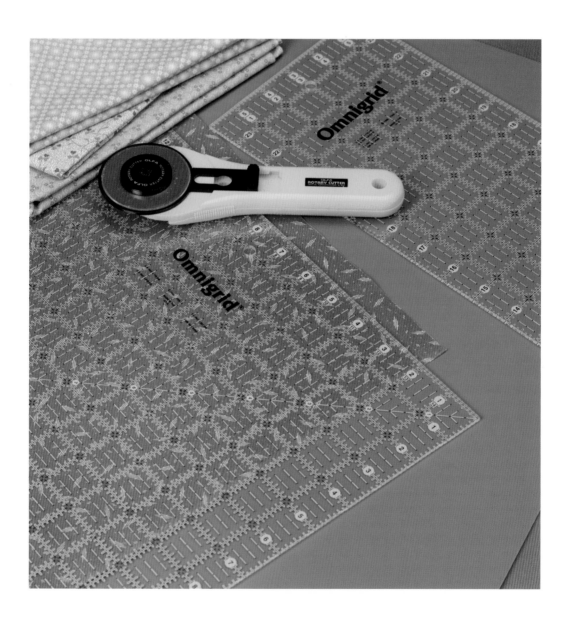

CUTTING

Strips, Rectangles & Squares

A simple tool that looks like a pizza cutter and has
revolutionized quilting is called a rotary cutter.
Instead of cutting fabric one piece at a time,
the rotary cutter allows you to cut long strips of fabric
and then crosscut those strips into the squares,
rectangles and triangles that make up most quilt tops.

The blade of a rotary cutter needs to be quite sharp
to cut through one or several layers of fabric.
It is important to follow the step-by-step photos
and safety tips for using a rotary cutter to cut the
fabric into strips for sewing the pieces of the quilt top.

Rotary Cutting

Always rotary cut fabric using a
self-healing cutting mat to protect your
work surface. Unprotected surfaces
will be permanently scarred, and you'll
dull the rotary cutter blade.

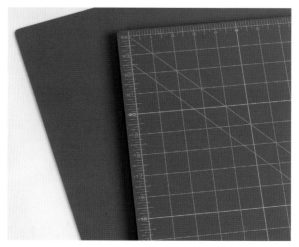

Do not depend on the rulers on the
sides of the cutting mat for accurate
measurements. Use the cutting mat's
gridlines only for positioning fabric. With
repeated rotary blade passes, gridlines
can become distorted.

*For accurate measurements always use
acrylic rulers instead of the preprinted
lines on a mat. Either side of a cutting
mat can be used for rotary cutting.*

What if...

*the ruler moves while you're rotary cutting? You may need to
cut a new straight edge. It's important to make the cut edge
as straight and accurate as possible.*

*you didn't apply enough pressure to the rotary cutter to
cleanly cut through both layers of fabric? Use your rotary
cutter again on those places.*

*you placed the fabric too near the left end of the mat
and the long ruler tipped off the edge of the mat? Reposition
the fabric so the entire long ruler is firmly positioned on the
mat for cutting.*

Squaring Up Fabric

SAFETY FIRST! The blades of a rotary cutter are very sharp, making them perfect for accurate cutting. Try out a variety of cutters to find one that feels good in your hand. All quality cutters have a safety mechanism to "close" the cutting blade when not in use. After each cut and before putting the rotary cutter down, close the blade. Soon this will become second nature to you and will prevent dangerous accidents. Always keep cutters out of the sight of children since rotary cutters may be tempting to play with if not closely guarded. When your blade is dull or nicked, change it. Damaged blades do not cut accurately and require extra effort that can also result in slipping and injury. Always cut away from yourself for safety.

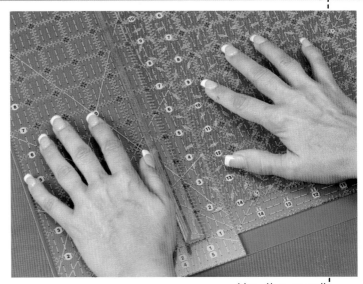

Use the small square ruler as a guide for positioning the long ruler.

Begin by folding the fabric in half lengthwise, matching the selvage edges as much as possible.

"Square up" the ends of your fabric before measuring and cutting pieces. This means that the cut edge of the fabric must be exactly perpendicular to the folded edge which creates a 90-degree angle. Align the

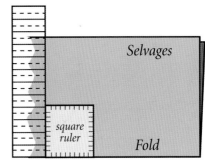

6 x 24" ruler

folded and selvage edges of the fabric with the lines on the cutting mat, and place a square acrylic ruler on the fold. Place a 6 x 24-inch acrylic ruler against the side of the square to get a 90-degree angle. Hold the ruler in place, remove the square, and cut along the edge of the long ruler. If you are left-handed, work from the opposite end of the fabric. Use the lines on your cutting mat to help line up fabric, but not to measure and cut strips. Use a ruler for accurate cutting, always checking to make sure your fabric is lined up with horizontal and vertical lines on the ruler.

Quick-Step: Fabric Straightening

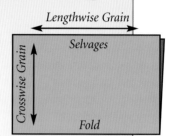

Lengthwise Grain
Selvages
Crosswise Grain
Fold

- Fold the fabric in half with the wrong sides together and selvages together.

- Work from the left raw edge of the fabric with the fold at the bottom.

- Align the small square ruler along the bottom fold *(photograph 1)*.

- Butt the right side of the long ruler to the left side of the small ruler *(photograph 1)*.

- Slide away the small square ruler. Rotary cut along the right side of the long ruler *(photograph 2)*.

- Roll the cutter as your fingers "walk" steadily from the bottom to the top *(photograph 3)*.

- Roll the cutter in a vertical position making sure the blade does not tip to the side *(photograph 4)*.

- Don't move the fabric.

- When you've successfully cut away the raw edge to make a straight edge, you're ready to cut strips according to your pattern instructions.

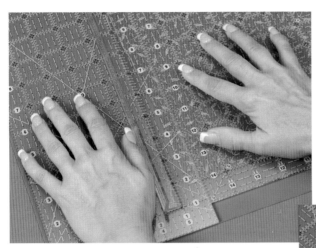

1 Use the small square ruler as a guide for positioning the long ruler.

2 Begin rotary cutting at the fold, always rolling the cutter away from you.

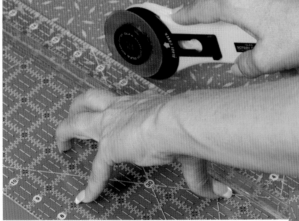

3 "Walk" your fingertips up the ruler, rolling the rotary cutter parallel to your fingers.

TIP:

There are various safety shields available in several sizes to guard your fingers from the sharp rotary cutter blades.

4 Roll the rotary cutter in a vertical position making sure the blade does not tip to the side.

TIP:

When cutting strips or rectangles, cut on the crosswise grain. Strips can then be cut into squares or smaller rectangles.

Generally, binding strips are cut on the crosswise grain unless the quilt has curved edges. If the quilt has curved edges or you are using a plaid or a check you will want to cut bias binding strips (refer to page 70 for Cutting Bias Strips).

If your strips are not straight after cutting a few of them, refold the fabric, align the folded and selvage edges with the lines on the cutting mat and "square off" the edge again by trimming to straighten, and begin cutting.

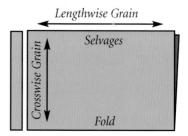

Lengthwise Grain

Crosswise Grain

Selvages

Fold

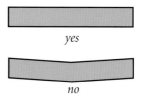

yes

no

Cutting the Strips

Cutting fabric into strips is most easily done with rotary cutting tools. First straighten the left edge of the fabric according to instructions that begin on page 28. Then, use the 6 x 24-inch ruler and the rotary cutter to cut fabric strips in the width needed for your quilt project.

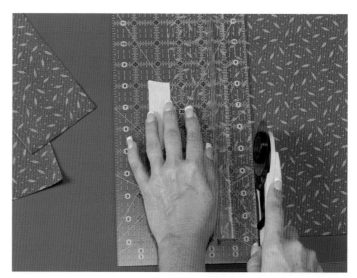

Use a piece of masking tape on the ruler as a reminder of the fabric strip width you're cutting— this strip measures 3-1/2-inches.

Crosscutting the Strips

When the fabric strips for your project have been cut, you're ready for crosscutting each strip into a smaller size using the rulers and the rotary cutter.

Begin by straightening the left edge of the fabric strip to remove the selvage as shown at right.

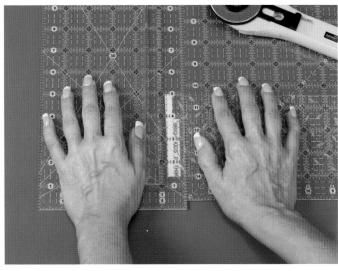

Always begin crosscutting the fabric by straightening the fabric strip's left edge. Here the selvage is being removed.

Use a small square ruler or the 6 x 24-inch ruler to crosscut the fabric strip into smaller units as shown at right. These will be the squares and rectangles you'll use for assembling the quilt top for the Jiffy Quilts projects that begin on page 72. The long strips will be used for the borders and binding strips.

Use the ruler to crosscut a 3-1/2-inch fabric strip into 3-1/2-inch squares. Note that masking tape is used as a quick visual guide to indicate the measurement on the ruler for the 3-1/2-inch square.

SEWING

Straight Seams,
Strip Sets & Borders

Since all the seam allowances that make up your quilt top
need to be accurate, discover how easy it is to set up your
machine with simple techniques for successful sewing.

Use the helpful tips for determining an accurate 1/4-inch
seam allowance and practice sewing straight seams.

After sewing the layered strips together, you'll press the
strips and then add the inner and outer borders.
In no time at all, the many pieces of your quilt top
will be assembled and ready for finishing.

Determining a 1/4-inch Seam Allowance

Accurate cutting and sewing straight seams are the most important part of the quiltmaking process. To determine an accurate 1/4-inch seam allowance on your machine, use the following method.

Use a piece of 1/4-inch graph paper, stitch along the 1/4-inch line as if the paper was fabric. Make note of where the edge of the paper lines up with your presser foot or on the throat plate of your machine. (Many quilters place a piece of painter's blue masking tape on the throat plate as a visual aid for guiding the edge of the fabric.) Practice your seam allowance with fabric.

Use a strip of 1/4-inch gridded graph paper to locate the 1/4-inch seam allowance position. Mark it with a piece of painter's blue masking tape or a short stack of Post-it® notes placed adjacent to the graph paper.

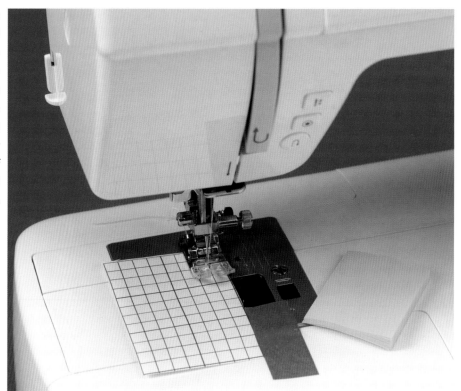

Sewing Practice Seams

For sewing straight seams, place right sides of the fabric pieces together and use 1/4-inch seam allowances throughout the entire quilt top unless otherwise stated in the directions.

Cut 2, 2-1/2 x 4-1/2-inch rectangles, place right sides together and stitch with a 1/4-inch seam allowance along one edge.

Press seam allowance in one direction and measure. At this point the unit should measure 4-1/2-inches square. If it does not, adjust your stitching guidelines and test again.

NOTE: *Seam allowances are included in the cutting sizes given in this book.*

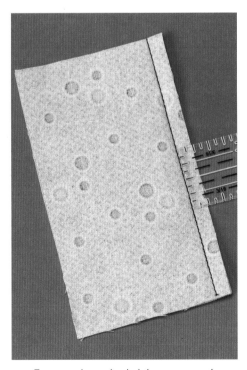

For sewing straight seams, place right sides of the fabric pieces together and use a 1/4-inch seam allowance.

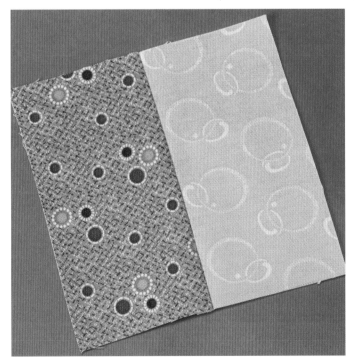

Your finished practice square should measure 4-1/2 x 4-1/2-inches. If it does not, adjust your stitching guidelines and test again. Practice makes perfect.

Sewing Layered Strips Together

Lay a strip on top of another, right sides together, carefully lining up the raw edges and sew using a 1/4-inch seam allowance. Be careful not to stretch the strips as you sew them together.

Lay a strip on top of another, right sides together, carefully lining up the raw edges and sew using a 1/4-inch seam allowance. You may want to pin layers together with straight pins perpendicular to seam line.

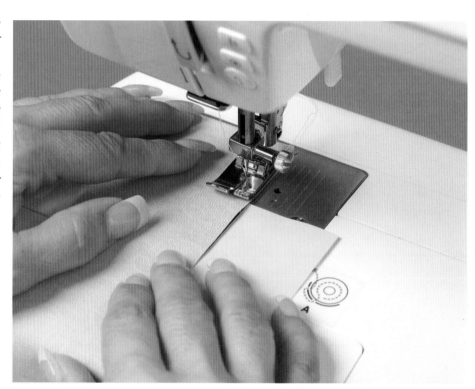

Use a short stack of Post-it® notes as your guide to an accurate 1/4-inch seam.

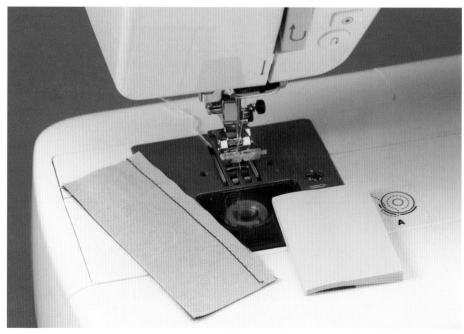

Pressing Strip Sets

When sewing strips of fabric together for strip sets, it is important to press the seam allowances nice and flat, usually toward the darker fabric.

Be careful not to stretch as you press, causing a "rainbow effect." This will affect the accuracy and shape of the pieces cut from the strip set. I like to press on the wrong side first and with the strips perpendicular to the ironing board. Then I flip the piece over and press on the right side to prevent little pleats from forming at the seams.

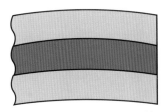

Avoid this rainbow effect

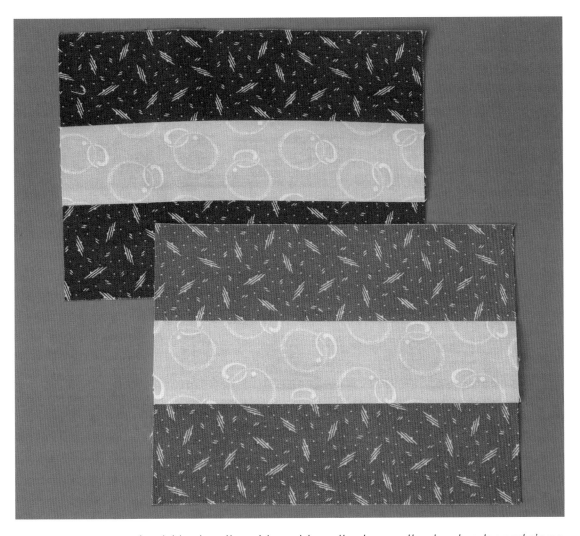

Avoid laying the strip set lengthwise on the ironing board since this seems to encourage the rainbow effect as shown above.

Helpful Hints for Sewing with Flannel

Always prewash and machine dry flannel. This will prevent severe shrinkage after the quilt is made. Some flannels shrink more than others. Treat the more heavily napped side of solid flannels as the right side of the fabric.

Because flannel stretches more than other cotton calicos and because the nap makes the quilt thicker, the design should be simple. Let the fabric and color make the design statement.

Use a 10- to 12-stitches per inch setting on your machine and a 1/4-inch seam allowance for piecing with flannel.

When sewing triangle-pieced squares together, take extra care not to stretch the diagonal seam. Trim off the points from the seam allowances to eliminate bulk. Press gently to prevent stretching pieces out of shape.

Check block measurements as you progress. "Square up" the blocks as needed since flannel will shift and the end result may be blocks that are misshapen. If you notice a piece of the flannel stretching more than the others, place it on the bottom when stitching on the machine. The natural action of the feed dogs will help prevent stretching.

Before stitching pieces, strips or borders together, pin often to prevent fabric from stretching and moving. When stitching longer pieces together, divide the pieces into quarters and pin. Divide into even smaller sections for more control.

NOTE: *When layering a flannel quilt top, use a lightweight batting to prevent the quilt from becoming too heavy.*

Borders

NOTE: *Cut borders to the width called for. Always cut border strips a few inches longer than needed, just to be safe. Diagonally piece the border strips together as needed (see page 67).*

1. With pins, mark the center points along all 4 sides of the quilt. For the top and bottom borders, measure the quilt from left to right through the middle.

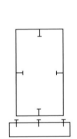

2. Measure and mark the border lengths and center points on the strips cut for the borders before sewing them on.

3. Pin the border strips to the quilt and stitch a 1/4-inch seam. Press the seam allowances toward the border. Trim off excess border lengths.

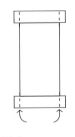

Trim away excess fabric

4. For the side borders, measure your quilt from top to bottom, including the borders just added, to determine the length of the side borders.

5. Measure and mark the side border lengths as you did for the top and bottom borders.

6. Pin and stitch the side border strips in place. Press and trim the border strips even with the borders just added.

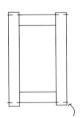

Trim away excess fabric

7. If your quilt has multiple borders, measure, mark and sew additional borders to the quilt in the same manner.

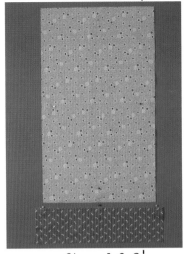

Steps 1 & 2
Mark center points with pins

Step 3
Trim away excess fabric

Step 6
Trim away excess fabric

PIECING

Blocks & Pressing

Now that you've mastered the art of sewing straight
seams, you'll soon see the results of your cutting
and sewing come to life as you assemble all the pieces
into a unit referred to as the quilt top. Piecing the squares,
rectangles and triangles together into blocks and then the
blocks together to complete the quilt top
is quite satisfying and is one of my favorite pastimes.

Piecing a Four-Patch Block

The four-patch, made of four same-size squares, is probably the simplest of all the pieced blocks. It can act as a block on its own or as the basis for a multitude of other blocks. Most often it is constructed of two fabrics with a strong contrast.

Cut two contrasting fabric strips the same width and sew them together.

Cut two contrasting fabric strips the same width. With right sides facing, use a 1/4-inch seam allowance to sew the long edges of the strips together to make a strip set. Press the seam allowances toward the darker fabric.

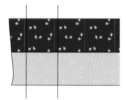

Square up one end of the strip set and cut two segments the same width as the original fabric strips.

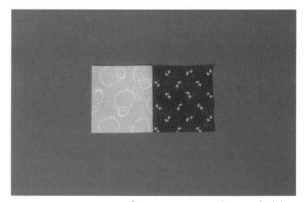

Square up edge of strips and cut 2-1/2-inch wide segments.

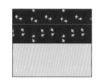

To complete the four-patch, sew segments together along one long edge, carefully matching seams and positioning the segments so the fabrics alternate. Press the seam allowance, either direction is okay.

Sew the segments together, carefully matching the seams and positioning the segments so the fabrics alternate. Press the seam allowance.

Piecing a Triangle Square

The basic triangle square may be used on its own as a quilt block or as a part of a more intricately-pieced block.

Cut two same-size squares of contrasting fabric and layer the squares with right sides together.

(**RED** *fabric is under* **BEIGE**)

Cut layered squares in half diagonally to make two sets of triangles.

Handle the triangles carefully as the diagonal edge is cut on the bias and easily stretches out of shape. Stitch 1/4-inch from the diagonal edge of each pair of triangles.

Press the seam allowances toward the darker triangle.

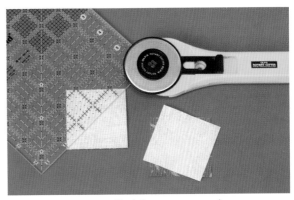

*Cut two same-size squares
of contrasting fabric.*

*Stitch 1/4-inch from the diagonal
edge of each pair of triangles.*

*Press the seam allowances
toward the darker triangle.*

Piecing a Pinwheel Block

The pinwheel, made of eight same-size triangles, is one of the more popular blocks. It is usually constructed with two contrasting fabrics. There are endless variations, many of which substitute small triangles for the larger triangles and use three or more fabrics. One variation is the double pinwheel used in Pinwheel Twist on page 106.

Cut two same-size squares each from two contrasting fabrics. Layer the squares with right sides together, using one of each fabric. Cut the layered squares in half diagonally to make four sets of triangles.

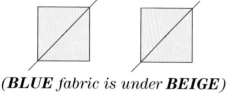

(BLUE fabric is under BEIGE)

Handle the triangles carefully as the diagonal edge is cut on the bias and easily stretches out of shape. Sew 1/4-inch from the diagonal edge of each pair of triangles.

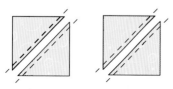

Press the seam allowances toward the darker fabric.

Arrange the triangle-pieced squares in two rows of two squares, alternating the fabric.

Sew the pieced squares together in rows with right sides facing, using a 1/4-inch seam allowance. Press the seam allowances toward the darker fabric.

To complete the pinwheel, sew the rows together, carefully matching the seams. Press the seam allowances in one direction. Either direction is okay, or to eliminate bulk this seam can be pressed open.

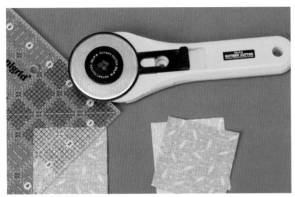

1 Cut the layered squares in half diagonally to make four sets of triangles.

4 Arrange the triangle squares in two rows of two squares, alternating the fabric.

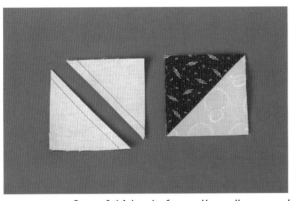

2 Sew 1/4-inch from the diagonal edge of each pair of triangles.

5 Sew the pieced squares together in rows with right sides facing, using a 1/4-inch seam allowance.

3 Press the seam allowances toward the darker fabric.

6 Sew the rows together, carefully matching the seams. Press the seam allowances in one direction, or to eliminate bulk, the seams can be pressed open.

TIP:

*Pressing seam
allowances in
one direction is
thought to create
a stronger seam.*

Pressing Seams

A general rule is to press all seam allowances toward the darker fabric. This prevents the seam allowances from showing through the lighter fabric on the front of the quilt. There are some exceptions to this rule, most often when multiple pieces come together at the same spot. In these cases, you may need to press the seam allowances in another direction or open to make the block lie flat. If it is necessary to press the seam allowances toward the lighter fabric, slightly trim the darker seam allowance so it is narrower than the lighter one.

When two seams will be joined together, press the seam allowances in opposite directions. When the rows are placed right sides together to be sewn, the pressed seams will abut, evenly distributing the bulk of the seam allowance. This also aids in matching pieces within blocks and helps to align rows of blocks in a quilt top.

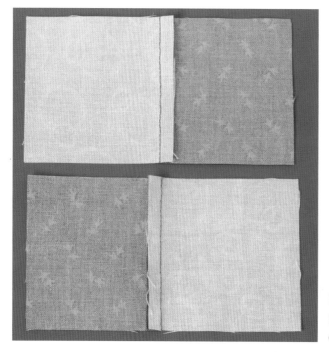

Pressing Direction

Pressing Direction

When two seams will be joined together, press the seam allowances in opposite directions.

Squaring Up Blocks

To square up your blocks, first check the seam allowances—often the source of any problem you may experience. It is always best to alter within the block rather than trim the outer edges. Next, make sure you have pressed accurately. Sometimes a block can become distorted by ironing instead of pressing.

To trim up block edges, use one of the many clear acrylic square rulers available on the market. Determine the center of the block; mark with a pin if needed. Lay the clear acrylic square over the block and align as many perpendicular and horizontal lines as you can to the seams in your block. This will indicate where the block is off.

Do not trim all off on one side; this usually results in distortion of the pieces in the block and the block design. Take a little off all sides until the block is square. When assembling many blocks, it is necessary to make sure all are the same size.

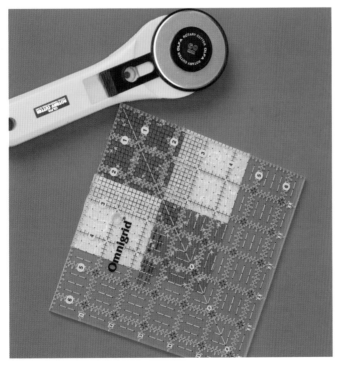

To square up your blocks, lay the clear acrylic square over the block and align as many perpendicular and horizontal lines as you can to the seams in your block.

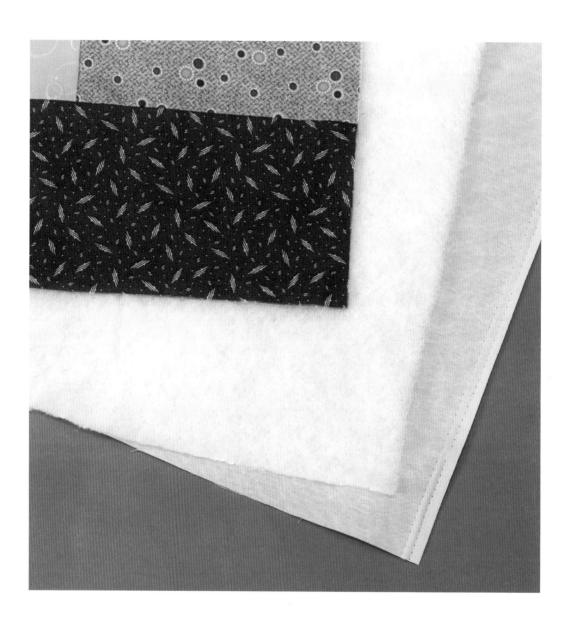

LAYERING

Quilt Top, Batting & Backing

After you've added the borders to your quilt center, you'll have a completed quilt top. If you decide to tie your quilt, you will not need to decide on a quilting design. If you are planning to quilt the layers, now is the time to add the quilting design. You'll find tips and techniques for choosing a design, quilting suggestions and marking the quilting design on your quilt top.

After adding a design to the top for quilting, follow the helpful tips for choosing batting and sandwiching it between the quilt top and the backing. Use safety pins or long basting stitches to hold the layers together until you're ready to secure the layers with simple machine quilting, hand quilting or yarn ties.

TIP:
*Quilting
Suggestions*

*Repeat one of the
design elements in
the quilt as part of
the quilting design.*

*Two or three parallel
rows of echo quilting
outside an appliqué
piece will highlight
the shape.*

*Stipple or meander
quilting behind a
design or central
motif will make the
primary design
more prominent.*

*Look for quilting
designs that will
cover two or more
borders rather than
choosing separate
designs for each
individual border.*

*Quilting in-the-ditch
of seams is an
effective way to get
a project quilted
without a great
deal of time spent
marking the quilt top.*

Choosing a Quilting Design

Quilting is such an individual process that it is difficult to recommend designs for each quilt. There are hundreds of quilting stencils available at quilt shops. (Templates are used generally for appliqué shapes; stencils are used for marking quilting designs.) I have developed several Thimbleberries® Quilt Stencils for Quilting Creations that are appropriate for hand quilting and continuous machine quilting.

There are a few suggestions that may help you decide how to quilt your project, depending on how much time you would like to spend quilting. Many quilters now use professional long-arm quilting machines or hire someone skilled at running these machines to do the quilting. This, of course, frees up more time to piece quilt tops.

Outline Quilting

- OUTLINE QUILTING
  *follows the outline and
  accentuates a pieced or
  appliquéd block by stitching
  about 1/4-inch away from the
  seam line or edge of the appliqué
  shape. It requires no marking. This
  can be done by hand or machine.*

- IN-THE-DITCH QUILTING
  *is understated because it **nearly**
  disappears in the seam. The
  stitches are made just next to the
  seam line or along an appliqué
  edge. It requires no marking and
  is a good choice for machine
  quilting or hand quilting.*

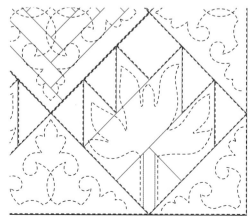

In-the-Ditch Quilting

- BACKGROUND QUILTING (crosshatch or grid design) *fills large spaces and puts more emphasis on the quilt patterns by making them stand out from the background. Background quilting can be done in straight lines or in a random pattern. This can be done by hand or machine.*

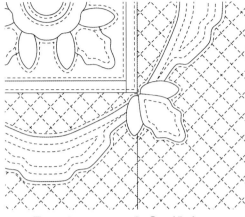

Background Quilting

- STIPPLE QUILTING (meandering) *requires no marking to create the random curves that flow across a quilt surface or fill areas of a quilt (that may already have a design) with concentrated quilting stitches. The goal is to avoid having the stitches cross over one another. This is rarely done by hand.*

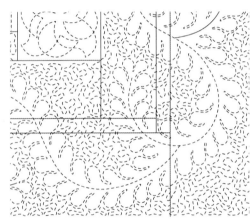

Stipple Quilting

- DESIGN QUILTING *is often a decorative accent in its own right. Popular designs include feathers, wreaths, cables, and swags which work well in open spaces such as large corner blocks or borders. This can be done by hand or machine.*

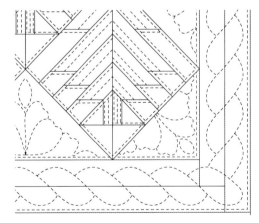

Design Quilting

- ECHO QUILTING *highlights a motif—usually an appliqué piece. Once the motif is outlined, two or three parallel rows of stitching are added at regular intervals. This can be done by hand or machine.*

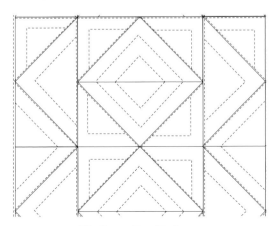

Echo Quilting

Marking the Quilting Design

Press the quilt top a final time before marking. When marking the quilt top, use a marking tool that will be visible on the quilt fabric and yet will be easy enough to remove. Always test your marking tool on a scrap of fabric before marking the entire quilt.

Along with a multitude of commercial marking tools available, you may find that very thin slivers of hand soap (Dial, Ivory, etc.) work well for marking medium to dark color fabrics. The thin lines of soap show up nicely and they are easily removed by simply rubbing gently with a piece of like-colored fabric. To remove the blue lines of water erasable markers, refer to the manufacturer's directions before laundering or pressing your finished quilt. Do not iron over marked lines before removing. Ironing markings on some materials will set the marks permanently.

Depending on the colors in your quilt top, use one or more of these notions to mark your quilting design: (top to bottom) Quilt Pounce™, a chalk-o-liner, a blue water erasable marker, marking pencils and a Chubby Crayon.

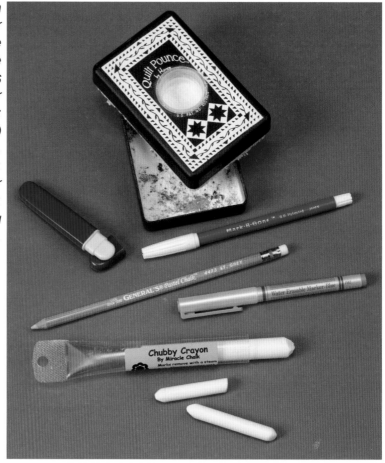

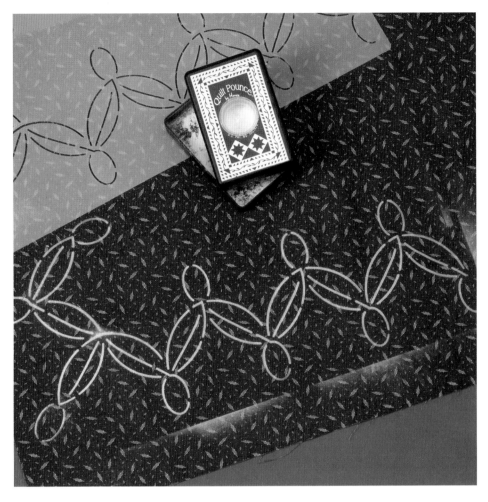

TIP:

*Keep your pressed
and marked quilt
top wrinkle-free
by folding it wrong
side out and
hanging it from a
skirt hanger.*

Pouncing the Quilting Design

After you've selected a quilting design, the Quilt Pounce™
makes it easy to transfer any size or variety of stencil to your
quilt top. Simply fill the Quilt Pounce™ pad's large inner
reservoir with the chalk powder (included) and gently wipe it
across the surface of the stencil that has been positioned on
the quilt top. Continue moving the stencil and "pouncing" the
quilting design. Some white and blue chalks do not iron off—they
brush/wash off. If you don't plan to wash your quilt, be sure to use
the iron-off Ultimate Quilt Pounce™.

TIP:

Batting is available
in several neutral
shades—white,
cream, charcoal
gray and black.

Batting

When you have completed your quilt top and are ready to layer and baste, you'll need a quilt batt and a backing fabric to make a quilt sandwich. Batting choices are nearly as varied as fabric choices. Several manufacturers have developed battings made from polyester and cotton, and blends of both. You can even find wool, silk, cashmere and alpaca in batting. Choose the batting that's right for your quilt by reading the label on the package.

Loft

Loft is the height or thickness of the batting. The denseness of fibers contribute to the batting's ultimate loft.

Choose a low-loft batting if you prefer a flatter appearance. Low-loft batting moves well beneath your sewing machine pressure foot when machine quilting.

NOTE: *For flannel, it is best to use a lightweight batting to prevent the finished quilt from becoming too heavy.*

Battings are available in a wide variety of choices—cotton, polyester or a blend of both shown above.

A batting's packaging information can tell you a lot about what it is, how it handles, and how to care for it.

TIP:

If you purchase batting that has been packaged in a tight roll, let it "air" before layering it in a quilt sandwich. To restore the loft, unwrap the batting and either allow it to lay out for several hours or briefly tumble it in the dryer on the air fluff setting.

Reading the Label

Read the quilt batting label for information about its suitability for quilting by machine, hand or tying. Batting for tying should indicate that it's okay to place ties 3- to 4-inches apart. Some battings permit ties or stitches from 6- to 8-inches apart. If you're not sure, ask at your fabric shop for a recommendation. As with fabric, expect to invest a little more money in a higher quality product.

Cutting the Batting

For the quilt sandwich, the batting is usually cut using a measurement that is several inches larger than the quilt top to allow for "wiggle room" when centering the quilt top. For example, a 36 x 48-inch quilt top would require a piece of batting that is 42 x 54-inches.

NOTE: *Excess batting and backing fabric will be trimmed away before the binding is added.*

Choosing the Backing

The backing of any quilt is just as important to the overall design as the pieced patchwork top. Combine large-scale prints or piece coordinating fabrics together to create an interesting quilt back. Using large pieces of fabric (perhaps three different prints that are the same length as the quilt) or a large piece of fabric that is bordered by compatible prints, keeps the number of seams to a minimum, which speeds up the process. The new 108-inch-wide fabric sold on the bolt eliminates the need for seaming entirely. Carefully selected fabrics for a well-constructed backing not only complement a finished quilt, but make it more useful as a reversible accent.

Crib—45 x 60-inches

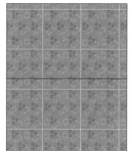

2-3/4 yards
Cut 2, 1-3/8 yard lengths

Twin—72 x 90-inches

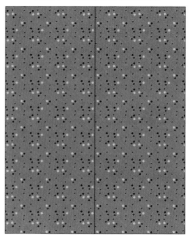

5-1/3 yards
Cut 2, 2-2/3 yard lengths

Double/Full—81 x 96-inches

7-1/8 yards
Cut 3, 2-3/8 yard lengths

Queen—90 x 108-inches

8 yards
Cut 3, 2-2/3 yard lengths

Preparing to Layer

When you've completed pressing and marking your quilt top for machine quilting, settled on a batting and prepared a backing, you're ready to make your quilt sandwich.

You'll Need

A hard surface work area, at least as large as the quilt backing. A large table or clean floor will work.

- BOTTOM LAYER—*the cut and pressed backing fabric that measures several inches larger than the quilt top*

- FILLER LAYER—*the batting that measures several inches larger than the quilt top*

- TOP LAYER—*the pressed quilt top with all seams laying flat*

Before you start building your "sandwich," be sure the backing fabric has been well-pressed so it will lay flat. Then, with the wrong side of the fabric facing up, lay the backing on the work surface. Smooth the fabric from the center outward. Avoid pulling the fabric too taut. Use small pieces of masking tape to securely fasten the backing to the work surface.

Center the batting on top of the quilt backing, smoothing it from the center outward.

Position the quilt top (right side up) on the batting and center and smooth it as you did with the batting.

With the wrong side of the fabric facing up, lay the backing on the work surface and secure with masking tape.

Center the batting on top of the quilt backing, smoothing it from the center outward.

Position the quilt top (right side up) on the batting and center and smooth it as you did with the batting.

Basting the Quilt Sandwich

As a first-time quiltmaker, you have two basting options. One method uses 1-inch to 1-1/2-inch (size 1 or size 2) nickel-plated safety pins. The other method uses items you probably already have— a needle and thread. Both have the same result: holding the layers together until the quilt sandwich is tied or quilted.

Use safety pins when you expect to complete quilting quickly by machine quilting or tying. Use needle and thread basting when you expect to hand quilt—a quilting process that takes more time. **NOTE:** *Over a long period of time, safety pins left in a quilt top may leave marks or small holes on the quilt.* With either method, work from the center of the quilt sandwich outward. Begin with a horizontal line and a vertical line through the center of the quilt sandwich to form quadrants on the quilt top.

Continue adding basting lines about 4-inches apart over the surface of the quilt to create a grid. Depending on the size of your project, you may want to complete one quadrant at a time.

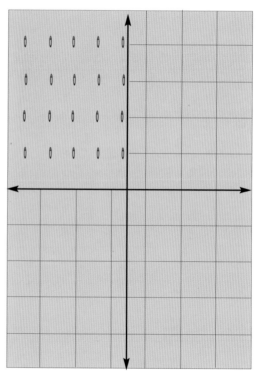

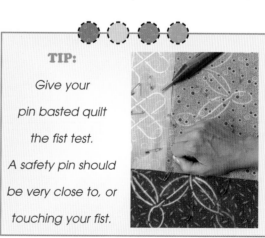

TIP:

Give your pin basted quilt the fist test.

A safety pin should be very close to, or touching your fist.

For pin basting, use 1-inch to 1-1/2-inch safety pins. Insert an opened pin into the quilt top with your dominant hand, going through all layers of the quilt sandwich. Close the safety pin with both hands, or use a grapefruit spoon or a Kwik Klip™. Position the pins approximately 4-inches apart to completely cover the quilt top. To save time, avoid placing pins in the locations where you intend to quilt or tie.

An easy method to test whether you have basted with enough safety pins is to place your fist anywhere on the quilt top. A safety pin should be very near or even touching each side of your fist.

For hand basting, thread a long darning needle with thread and make stitches about 2-inches long through all layers of the quilt sandwich. Space the rows of basting lines about 4-inches apart. If the project is large,

The Kwik Klip™ is held in the left hand and used to lift the safety pin tip to the safety pin head.

many quilters will add diagonal hand basting lines radiating out from the center before thread basting the grid lines in the quadrants.

TIP:

If your quilting project is small, consider using a basting spray instead of safey pins or thread basting. The spray temporarily holds the layers of the quilt sandwich together and works well for table runners and wallhangings. Follow the manufacturer's directions carefully and work in a well ventilated area.

FINISHING

Quilting, Binding & Hanging

After you've marked your completed quilt top with
quilting designs, layer it with the batting and backing to
make a sandwich temporarily secured by safety pins or
long basting stitches. Then, you're ready to quilt the layers
by hand or machine or simply add yarn ties.

Machine quilting can be quite easy and gets faster results.
Hand quilting is more precise and allows you greater
control over the length of your stitches. The small projects in
this book are perfect for beginning to learn either method.
On the following pages you'll find the basics of machine
and hand quilting. You may choose to combine quilting
methods, using machine quilting in the borders
and hand quilting in the blocks of your quilt.

Finishing your quilt or runner is as easy as adding
the binding, an optional sleeve for hanging
and a personalized label, if desired.

Follow the easy instructions on the next few pages, and in
no time at all you'll have successfully finished your first quilt.

TIP:

When you begin a line of machine quilting, take several stitches in the same place, then gradually lengthen the stitch, taking several stitches very close together before lengthening the stitch to 8 to 12 stitches per inch. Use these stitches at the beginning and end of quilting to help secure the threads.

Straight-Line Quilting

With a little practice you can successfully straight-line quilt with your sewing machine. Using a walking or even-feed foot ensures that the quilt top and the backing fabric move through the sewing machine at the same rate. The grippers on the bottom of the walking foot work with the machine's feed dogs to sew through the thickness of multiple layers. Check to see if it is a built-in feature of your machine, if not, you may choose to purchase the walking foot.

It is also possible to straight-line quilt without a walking foot. It just takes more attention to keeping the layers of fabric and batting taut to prevent wrinkles. The walking foot can be of real help.

To begin machine quilting, adjust your stitch length to the shortest length on your machine and sew for about 1/4-inch. Change the stitch length to 8- to 12-stitches per inch and continue machine quilting. Finish by returning to the shortest stitch length and sew the final 1/4-inch. Use this technique to start and stop each line of machine quilting. Starting and stopping with small stitches prevents the stitching from coming undone. Start by quilting straight lines and as you gain confidence advance to more detailed quilting designs.

Free-Motion Quilting

Free-motion quilting is used to create curved random lines. Using a darning foot with the machine's feed dogs down allows you to move your project in any direction. Use your hands to glide the fabric layers in the desired direction. Try to maintain a constant speed on your machine. You control the length of the stitch as you move your quilt. Moving it slowly results in shorter stitches and moving it fast results in longer stitches. Start and stop your quilting with several small stitches made very close together. Be patient, as small consistent stitches will take practice.

Darning Foot

Walking Foot

Hand Quilting

Small, evenly spaced stitches are the trademark of hand quilting. A beginner should strive for evenly spaced, uniform-size stitches. Quilting stitches will usually decrease in size as you practice and gain experience.

Wooden hoops or plastic frames are often used to hold quilt layers together for hand quilting, keeping them smooth and evenly taut. A screw and bolt attached to the outer circle of the hoop are used to tighten it around the three layers of the quilt. It is moved from one area of the quilt to another as quilting is completed. The layers of a quilt should be basted together before inserting them into a hoop or frame so they won't shift.

Hand quilters most often use a size 10 between needle and 100 percent cotton quilting thread.

Thread your needle with an 18-inch length of quilting thread and knot the end. Begin and end your stitching by burying the thread tail between the layers of the quilt. This will prevent knots from showing on the front or back of the quilt.

A quilt hoop is a small, two-part "frame" used to hold the layers of a quilt together. It keeps the tension even and prevents the quilt layers from slipping while being quilted. Most hoops are made of wood and are either circular, oval or square.

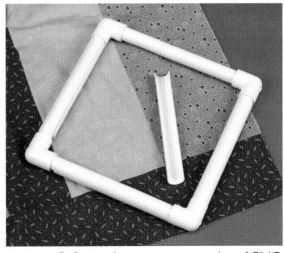

Q-Snap frames are made of PVC plastic and are easily snapped together for quilting and disassembled for storage or traveling. These frames are available in square or rectangular shapes.

Insert your needle into the quilt through the quilt top and batting a few inches from where you want to begin quilting. Do not insert your needle into the backing. Bring the needle back to the surface in position to make the first stitch. Tug gently on the thread to pop the knot through the quilt top and embed it in the batting.

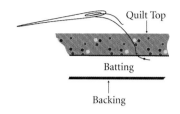

Tug gently on the thread to pop the knot through the quilt top and embed it in the batting.

Running Stitch

For this standard hand quilting stitch, you will want to wear a thimble on the middle finger of your stitching hand.

Hold the needle between your thumb and index finger. Place your other hand under the quilt, with the tip of your index finger on the spot where the needle will come through the quilt back. With the needle angled slightly away from you, push the needle through the layers until you feel the tip of the needle beneath the quilt.

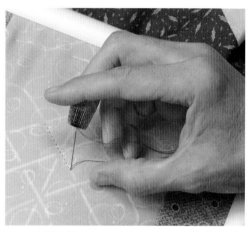

With the needle angled slightly away from you, push the needle through the layers until you feel the tip of the needle beneath the quilt.

When you feel the needle tip, slide your finger underneath the quilt toward you, pushing up against the inside of the needle to help return it to the top. At the same time, with your top hand roll the needle away from you. Gently push the needle forward and up through the quilt layers until the amount of the needle showing is the length you want the next stitch to be.

Lift the eye of the needle with your thimble finger, positioning your thumb just ahead of the

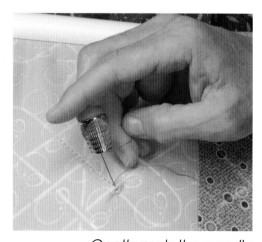

Gently push the needle forward and up through the quilt layers until the amount of the needle showing is the length you want the next stitch to be.

stitching. Rock the eye of the needle upward until the needle is almost perpendicular to the quilt top and the tip is in the fabric. Push down on the needle until you feel the tip beneath the quilt again.

As before, push the needle tip with your underneath finger and roll the eye of the needle down and forward with your thimble finger to return the needle tip to the top.

Pull the needle away from the quilt top until the stitches are snug. Keeping your stitches uniform in length is more important than the actual length of your individual stitches.

Ending

When the thread in your needle is about 6-inches long, you'll want to tie off the thread. One easy method is to make a circle with your thread and bring the needle up through that circle. Hold the circle down with your finger while reducing its size by pulling on the threaded needle to keep the knot from forming too soon. The idea is to get the knot to form about 1/4-inch from the quilt top so you have some length to bury the knot in the batting.

Insert the needle back into the same hole from which the thread is emerging. Jump the needle about 1/2-inch between the layers and bring it to the surface. Pop the knot between the layers and cut the thread close to the quilt top.

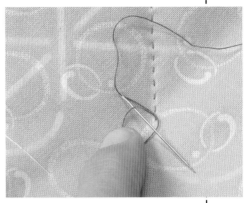

Hold the thread circle down with your finger. Reduce its size by pulling on the threaded needle to form a knot about 1/4-inch from the quilt top.

TIP:

Tying the Quilt

The technique for tying a quilt is a quick alternative to quilting. Begin tying the basted quilt at the center and work outward.

Thread a size 14 to 18 darning needle with an 18-inch single strand of perle cotton, embroidery floss or sport-weight yarn. Beginning and ending on the quilt top, make a single up-down stitch that is about 1/8-inch to 1/4-inch wide through all three layers of the quilt. Pull the thread or yarn through to leave a 3-inch tail at the end.

Place the second stitch in a crisscross fashion through all three layers, returning to the quilt top. Pull the threads tight. Trim the thread or yarn, leaving another 3-inch tail.

Tie the tails together in a square knot— right over left, left over right—as shown below. Trim the tails to approximately 1-inch.

Finishing the Quilt

In order to successfully finish your quilt, make sure you've followed the steps outlined in the previous chapters. You'll find the summarized finishing steps below.

1. Remove the selvages from the backing fabric. Sew the long edges together, and press. Trim the backing and batting so they are 4-inches to 6-inches larger than the quilt top.

2. Press the quilt top before marking. Mark the quilt top for quilting. Layer the backing, batting and quilt top. Baste the 3 layers together and quilt.

3. When quilting is complete, remove basting stitches or safety pins. Hand baste all 3 layers together a scant 1/4-inch from the edge. This hand basting keeps the layers from shifting and prevents puckers from forming when adding the binding. Trim excess batting and backing fabric even with the edge of the quilt top. Add the binding.

Cutting Binding Strips

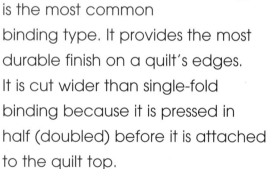

Double-fold or French-fold binding is the most common binding type. It provides the most durable finish on a quilt's edges. It is cut wider than single-fold binding because it is pressed in half (doubled) before it is attached to the quilt top.

For 1/2-inch-wide finished double-fold binding, cut 2-3/4-inch-wide binding strips. The binding strips for double-fold binding can be cut on the straight or bias grain. If you are binding a quilt with curved edges, cut your strips on the bias grain, see page 70.

Crosswise Grain Binding

For most quilts, binding strips may be cut on the straight grain. Use a fabric's crosswise straight grain rather than its lengthwise grain for more give and elasticity. If your quilt has curved edges, cut the strips on the bias (see page 70).

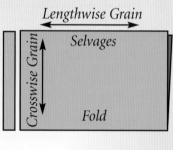

Cut crosswise strips the desired width, cutting enough strips to equal the total length needed.

Use a piece of masking tape on the ruler as a reminder of the fabric strip width you're cutting—this strip measures 2-3/4-inches.

Binding and Diagonal Piecing

1. Diagonally piece the binding strips.

Diagonal Piecing

*Stitch
diagonally*

*Trim to 1/4-inch
seam allowance*

*Press seam
open*

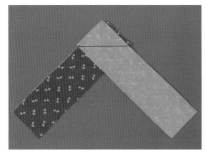
Stitch diagonally

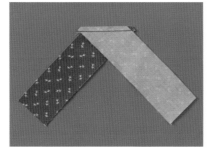
*Trim to 1/4-inch
seam allowance*

Press seam open

2. Fold the strip in half lengthwise, wrong sides together, and press.

Double-layer Binding

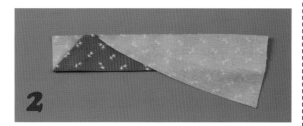

3. Unfold and trim one end at a 45-degree angle. Turn under the edge 1/4-inch and press. Refold the strip.

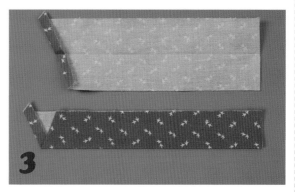

4. With raw edges of the binding and quilt top even, stitch with a **3/8-inch** seam allowance, starting 2-inches from the angled end.

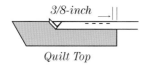
Quilt Top

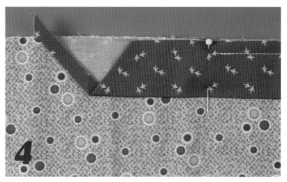

5. Miter the binding at the corners as follows. As you approach a corner of the quilt, stop sewing **3/8-inch** from the corner of the quilt.

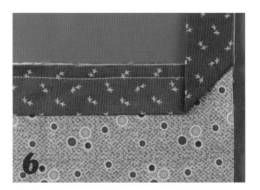

6. Clip the threads and remove the quilt from under the presser foot. Flip the binding strip up and away from the quilt, then fold the binding down even with the raw edge of the quilt. Begin sewing at the upper edge. Miter all 4 corners in this manner.

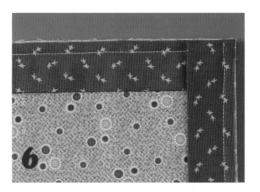

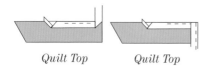

Quilt Top   *Quilt Top*

7. Trim the end of the binding so it can be tucked inside of the beginning binding 3/8-inch. Finish stitching the seam.

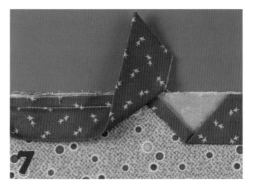

Quilt Back   *Quilt Back*

8. Turn the folded edge of the binding over the raw edges and to the back of the quilt so that the stitching line does not show. Hand sew the binding in place, folding in the mitered corners as you stitch.

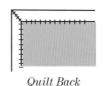

Quilt Back   *Quilt Back*   *Quilt Back*

Hand Sewing the Binding to the Back

Now you're ready to hand sew the binding into place.

Take care at each corner to fold and tuck fabric into mitered corner as shown at right.

For hand sewing the binding, use quilting thread to give your hand stitches extra strength. Or, use a thread that's a slightly heavier weight than the thread used to piece the quilt. For example, if you used a 50-weight piecing thread, use a 40-weight thread for binding.

Turn the folded edge of the binding to the quilt back, aligning the fold with the machine stitches. Use 3 to 4 silk pins at a time to hold the binding in place. Remove pins as you sew.

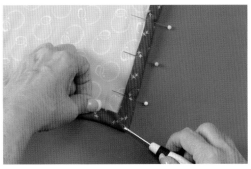

Make sure the binding is tucked into a fold to form a 45-degree mitered corner.

Mitered corners on the front and back of the quilt should look the same.

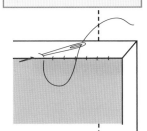

Cutting Bias Strips

If a quilt has curved edges it will require bias binding. Bias binding will "give" or stretch making it possible to go around curves.

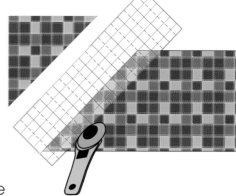

Crosswise Grain

True Bias

Lengthwise Grain

Selvage

Selvage   *Crosswise Grain*

- Trim the yardage on the crosswise grain so the edges are straight. Do not cut away the selvages at this time.

- To cut bias strips, with the right side facing up, fold yardage on the diagonal. To do so, fold the selvage edge (lengthwise grain) over to meet the cut edge (crosswise grain), forming a triangle. This diagonal fold is the true bias.

- Position the ruler the desired strip width from the cut edge (2-3/4-inch for bindings unless otherwise stated) and cut a strip. Move the ruler across the fabric cutting parallel strips in the desired width.

- Sometimes bias binding is used because of the design of the fabric. For example, plaids and checks are best used on the bias creating a very nice design element and a much nicer binding when using plaids.

TIP:

*Personalize your
quilt with a
label that includes:*

• Name of your
Thimbleberries® Quilt

• Quiltmaker

• Month and year

*Cut label allowing
1/4-inch to be turned
under at the edges
and hand stitch
to quilt back.*

Adding a Label

Adding a Hanging Sleeve

To hang wall quilts, attach a casing that is made of the same fabric as the quilt back. Attach this casing at the top of the quilt, just below the binding. Often, it is helpful to attach a second casing at the bottom of the quilt so you can insert a dowel into it which will help weight the quilt and make it hang free of ripples.

To make a rod casing or "sleeve," cut enough strips of fabric equal to the width of the quilt plus 2-inches for side hems. Generally, 6-inch wide strips will accommodate most rods. If you are using a rod with a larger diameter, increase the width of the strips.

Seam the strips together to get the length needed; press. Fold the strip in half lengthwise, wrong sides together. Stitch the long raw edges together with a 1/4-inch seam allowance. Center the seam on the backside of the sleeve; press. The raw edges of the seam will be concealed when the sleeve is stitched to the back of the quilt. Turn under both of the short raw edges; press and stitch to hem the ends. The final measurement should be about 1-inch from the quilt's side edges. The cut length of the rod should be about 1/2-inch from the quilt's edge.

Pin the sleeve to the back of the quilt so the top edge of the sleeve is just below the binding. Hand stitch the top edge of the sleeve in place, then the bottom edge. Make sure to knot and secure your stitches at each end of the sleeve to make sure it will not pull away from the quilt with use. Slip the rod into the casing. If your wall quilt is not directional, making a sleeve for the bottom edge will allow you to turn your quilt end to end to relieve the stress at the top edge. You could also slip a dowel into the bottom sleeve to help anchor the lower edge of the wall quilt.

TIP:

A wooden yardstick, a piece of drilled hardwood, a medium diameter dowel rod with eyescrews or a small diameter dowel rod are useful as sleeve rods.

Secure rod to wall with nails through drilled holes or eye screws.

OR

Simply rest wood on nails eliminating the drilled holes or eye screws.

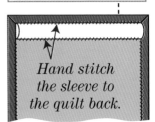

Hand stitch the sleeve to the quilt back.

JIFFY QUILTS™ PROJECTS

Now the fun begins as you choose a Jiffy Quilt or runner to make for the very first time. With names like Berry Sweet and Rainbow Sherbet, you'll discover a treat in store every time.

You'll find that some of the wall quilts and runners are shown in alternate colorways. Also, quilting guides are offered for some of the projects to give you confidence to begin quilting by machine or by hand. **NOTE:** *The seam allowances are included in the cutting sizes given in this book.*

Easy Does It Runner

24 x 40-inches

Materials

3/4 yard **RED PRINT**
for block centers and outer border

5/8 yard **BEIGE PRINT**
for block and dogtooth backgrounds

1/3 yard **YELLOW PRINT**
for dogtooth border

1/2 yard **BLACK PRINT**
for corner squares and binding

1-1/4 yards for backing

quilt batting, at least 30 x 46-inches

A rotary cutter, mat, and wide clear plastic
ruler with 1/8-inch markings are necessary
tools in attaining accuracy.

A 6 x 24-inch ruler is recommended

Runner Center

Jiffy Cutting for Runner Center

From **RED PRINT**:

- Cut 2, 4-1/2 x 42-inch strips.
    From the strips cut:
    6, 4-1/2 x 8-1/2-inch rectangles

From **BEIGE PRINT**:

- Cut 4, 4-1/2 x 42-inch strips.
    From the strips cut:
    28, 4-1/2-inch squares

From **YELLOW PRINT**:

- Cut 2, 4-1/2 x 42-inch strips.
    From the strips cut:
    8, 4-1/2 x 8-1/2-inch rectangles

From **BLACK PRINT**:

- Cut 1, 4-1/2 x 42-inch strip.
    From the strip cut:
    4, 4-1/2-inch corner squares

Jiffy Piecing

Step 1 With right sides together, position a 4-1/2-inch **BEIGE** square on the corner of a 4-1/2 x 8-1/2-inch **RED** rectangle. Draw a diagonal line on the square and stitch on the line. Trim the seam allowance to 1/4-inch; press. Repeat this process on the opposite corner of the rectangle.

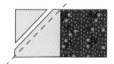

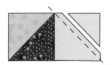

Make 6

Step 2 Sew the Step 1 units together in pairs; press. <u>At this point each block should measure 8-1/2-inches square.</u>

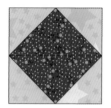

Make 3

Step 3 With right sides together, position a 4-1/2-inch **BEIGE** square on the corner of a 4-1/2 x 8-1/2-inch **YELLOW** rectangle. Draw a diagonal line on the square; stitch, trim, and press. Repeat this process on the opposite corner of the rectangle.

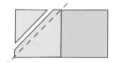

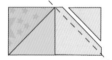

Make 8

Step 4 Sew 6 of the Step 3 units to both side edges of the Step 2 blocks; press. <u>At this point each unit should measure 8-1/2 x 16-1/2-inches.</u>

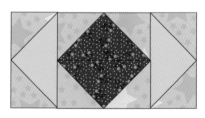

Make 3

Step 5 Referring to the diagram, sew together the Step 4 units; press. <u>At this point the runner center should measure 16-1/2 x 24-1/2-inches.</u>

Step 6 Sew the 4-1/2-inch **BLACK** corner squares to both ends of the remaining Step 3 units; press.

Make 2

Step 7 Referring to the runner diagram for block placement sew the Step 6 units to both ends of the quilt center; press. <u>At this point the runner center should measure 16-1/2 x 32-1/2-inches.</u>

Jiffy Outer Border

NOTE: *The yardage given allows for the border strips to be cut on the crosswise grain. Read through **Border** instructions on page 39 for general instructions on adding borders.*

Jiffy Cutting for Border

From **RED PRINT**:
- Cut 3, 4-1/2 x 42-inch outer border strips

Attaching the Outer Border

Attach the 4-1/2-inch wide **RED PRINT** outer border strips.

Putting It All Together

Trim the batting and backing so they are about 6-inches larger than the runner top. Refer to **Finishing the Quilt** on page 66 for complete instructions.

Jiffy Quilting Suggestions:

- The **RED** blocks - TB45 Star Heart.
- The **BEIGE** background - echo quilting.
- The **YELLOW** dogtooth border - echo quilting.
- The **BLACK** corner squares - large X.
- The **RED** outer border - channel quilt.

*The **THIMBLEBERRIES**® quilt stencils are by Quilting Creations International. To view the stencil designs, refer to page 78.*

Jiffy Binding

*NOTE: Refer to **Binding** on page 67 for complete instructions with detailed illustrations.*

Jiffy Cutting for Binding

From **BLACK PRINT**:

• Cut 4, 2-3/4 x 42-inch strips

Attaching the Binding

Step 1   Diagonally piece the strips together. Fold the strip in half lengthwise, wrong sides together; press.

Stitch diagonally   Trim to 1/4" seam allowance   Press seam open

Diagonal Piecing

Step 2   With raw edges of the binding and runner top even, stitch with a 3/8-inch seam allowance.

Step 3   Miter binding at the corners. To do so, stop sewing 3/8-inch from the corner of the runner top. Flip the binding strip up and away from the runner, then fold the binding down even with the raw edge of the runner. Begin sewing at the upper edge. Miter all 4 corners in this manner.

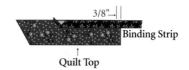

3/8"

Binding Strip

Quilt Top

Step 4   Bring the folded edge of the binding to the back of the runner and hand sew the binding in place.

Easy Does It Runner
Quilting Suggestion

Easy Does It Runner

24 x 40-inches

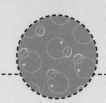

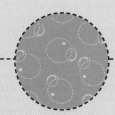
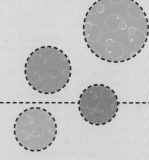

Berry Sweet

52 x 54-inches

Materials

1/2 yard **YELLOW BLOCK PRINT**
for quilt center

1/4 yard **YELLOW DOT**
for quilt center

3/8 yard **GREEN PRINT**
for quilt center

5/8 yard **BLUE ALPHABET PRINT**
for quilt center

1-1/8 yards **ROSE PRINT**
for quilt center and border

5/8 yard **GREEN PRINT**
for binding

3-1/4 yards **YELLOW BLOCK PRINT** (flannel)
for backing
OR
3-1/4 yards **CREAM FLORAL**
for backing

quilt batting, at least 58 x 60-inches

A rotary cutter, mat, and wide clear
plastic ruler with 1/8-inch markings are
necessary tools in attaining accuracy.

A 6 x 24-inch ruler is recommended

Jiffy Quilt Center

Jiffy Cutting for Quilt Center

From **YELLOW BLOCK PRINT**:
- Cut 2, 6-1/2 x 40-1/2-inch strips

From **YELLOW DOT**:
- Cut 1, 4-1/2 x 42-inch strip.
  From the strip cut:
  6, 4-1/2-inch squares

From **GREEN PRINT**:
- Cut 1, 6-1/2 x 40-1/2-inch strip
- Cut 1, 4-1/2 x 42-inch strip.
  From the strip cut:
  8, 4-1/2-inch squares

From **BLUE ALPHABET PRINT**:
- Cut 4, 4-1/2 x 40-1/2-inch strips

From **ROSE PRINT**:
- Cut 1, 4-1/2 x 42-inch strip.
  From the strip cut:
  6, 4-1/2-inch squares

Jiffy Piecing

Step 1 Referring to the diagram for placement, sew together 3 of the 4-1/2-inch **YELLOW DOT** squares, 4 of the 4-1/2-inch **GREEN** squares, and 3 of the 4-1/2-inch **ROSE** squares; press. Make 2 block rows. <u>At this point each block row should measure 4-1/2 x 40-1/2-inches.</u>

Make 2 block rows

Step 2 Sew the 4-1/2 x 40-1/2-inch **BLUE ALPHABET PRINT** strips to both side edges of the block rows; press. Make 2 pieced strips. <u>At this point each pieced strip should measure 12-1/2 x 40-1/2-inches.</u>

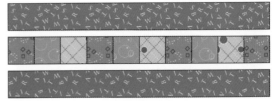

Make 2

Step 3 Sew the 6-1/2 x 40-1/2-inch **YELLOW BLOCK PRINT** strips to both side edges of the 6-1/2 x 40-1/2-inch **GREEN** strip; press. <u>At this point the center unit should measure 18-1/2 x 40-1/2-inches.</u>

Step 4 Referring to the quilt assembly diagram for placement, sew the Step 2 pieced strips to the top/bottom edges of the Step 3 center unit; press. <u>At this point the quilt center should measure 40-1/2 x 42-1/2-inches.</u>

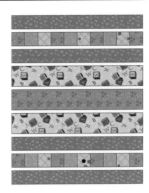

Quilt Assembly Diagram

Jiffy Border

NOTE: *The yardage given allows for the border strips to be cut on the crosswise grain. Diagonally piece the strips as needed, referring to **Diagonal Piecing** on page 67.*

Jiffy Cutting for Border

From **ROSE PRINT:**

- Cut 5, 6-1/2 x 42-inch border strips

Attaching the Borders

Step 1   With pins, mark the center points along all 4 sides of the quilt. For the top/bottom borders, measure the quilt from left to right through the middle. This measurement will give you the most accurate measurement that will result in a "square" quilt.

Step 2   Measure and mark the border lengths and center points on the 6-1/2-inch wide **ROSE** strips cut for the borders before sewing them on.

Step 3   Pin the border strips to the quilt matching the pinned points on each of the borders and the quilt. Stitch a 1/4-inch seam. Press the seam allowance toward the borders. Trim off excess border lengths.

Trim away excess fabric

Step 4   For the side borders, measure your quilt from top to bottom, including the borders just added, to determine the length of the side borders.

Step 5   Measure and mark the 6-1/2-inch wide **ROSE** side border lengths as you did for the top/bottom borders.

Step 6   Pin and stitch the side border strips in place; press and trim.

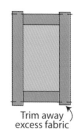

Trim away excess fabric

Putting It All Together

Step 1   Cut the 3-1/4 yard length of backing fabric in half crosswise to make 2, 1-5/8 yard lengths. Sew the long edges together; press. Trim the batting and backing so they are 3-inches larger on all sides than the quilt top.

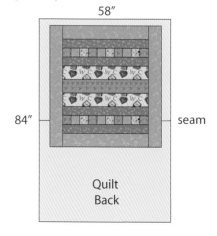

Finished Back Diagram

Step 2   Mark the quilt top for quilting. Layer the backing, batting, and quilt top. To secure the layers together for hand quilting, use long basting stitches by hand to hold the layers together. Quilt as desired.

Jiffy Quilting Suggestions:

- The **GREEN** strip - use TB25 Connecting Maze stencil.

- The **BLUE ALPHABET PRINT** strips - use TB37 Pansy Vine stencil, reduce as needed.

- The **ROSE** outer border - use TB29 Leaf Sketch stencil, reduce as needed.

- The **YELLOW ALPHABET PRINT** strips - meander.

The **THIMBLEBERRIES®** quilt stencils are by Quilting Creations International.

Step 3   When quilting is complete, hand baste the 3 layers together a scant 1/4-inch from the edge. This basting keeps the layers from shifting and prevents puckers from forming when adding the binding. Trim excess batting and backing fabric even with the edge of the quilt top.

Jiffy Binding

NOTE: *Refer to **Binding** on page 67 for complete binding instructions with detailed illustrations.*

Jiffy Cutting for Binding

From **GREEN PRINT:**

- Cut 6, 2-3/4 x 42-inch strips

Attaching the Binding

Step 1   Diagonally piece the strips together. Fold the strip in half lengthwise, wrong sides together; press.

Stitch diagonally   Trim to 1/4" seam allowance   Press seam open

Diagonal Piecing

Step 2   With raw edges of the binding and quilt top even, stitch with a 3/8-inch seam allowance.

Step 3   Miter binding at the corners. To do so, stop sewing 3/8-inch from the corner of the quilt. Flip the binding strip up and away from the quilt, then fold the binding down even with the raw edge of the quilt. Begin sewing at the upper edge. Miter all 4 corners in this manner.

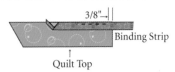

Quilt Top

Step 4   Bring the folded edge of the binding to the back of the quilt and hand sew the binding in place.

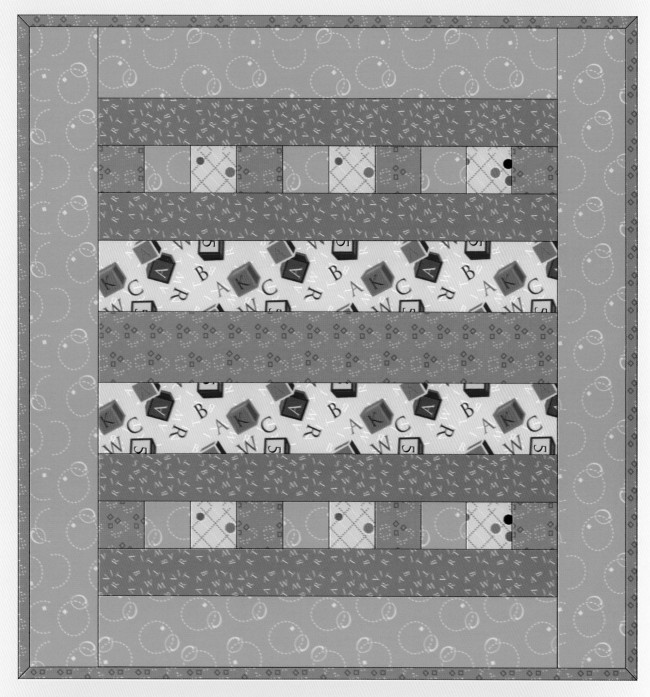

Berry Sweet
52 x 54-inches

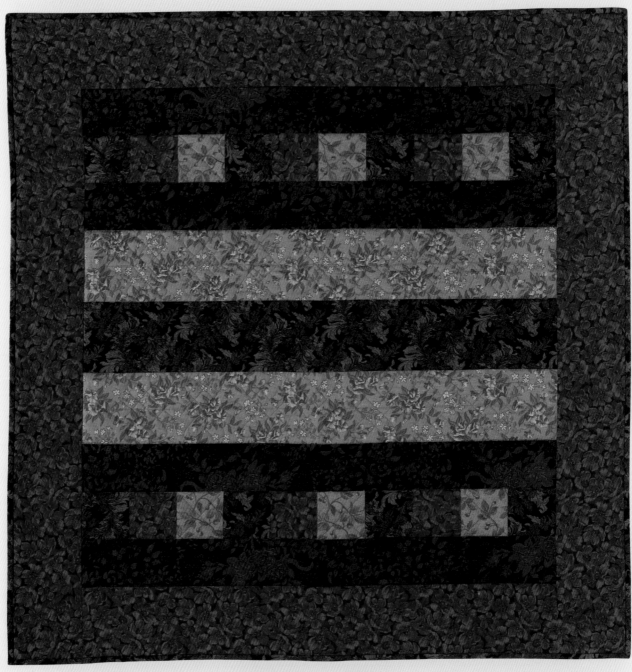

Sedona Sky

52 x 54-inches

Hollyberry
52 x 54-inches

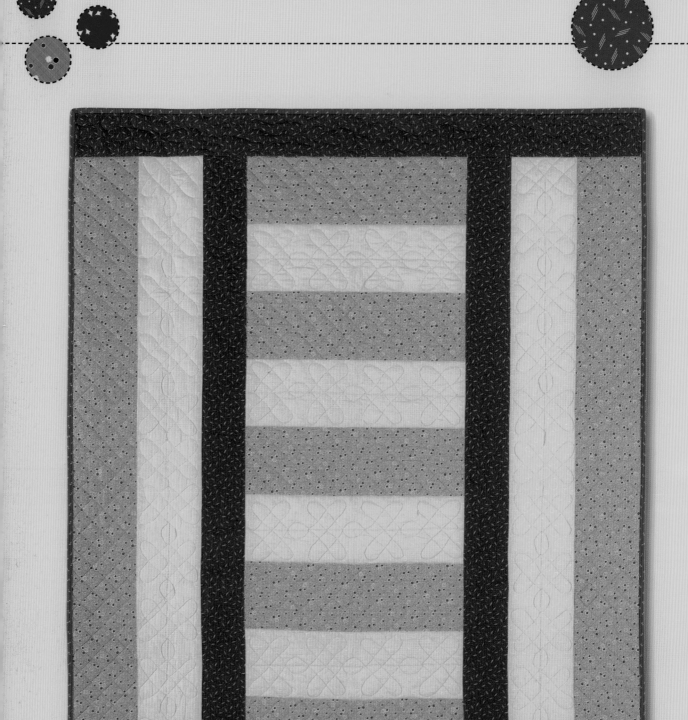

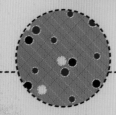

Blueberry Blue

52 x 62-inches

Materials

1-3/8 yards **BLUE DOT**
for quilt center and outer border

1-1/8 yards **YELLOW PRINT**
for quilt center and middle border

7/8 yard **BLUE PRINT**
for quilt center and outer border

5/8 yard **RED PRINT** for binding

3-1/4 yards **BLUE BLOCK PRINT** (flannel)
for backing
OR
3-1/4 yards **NAVY/GREEN DIAGONAL PRINT**
for backing

quilt batting, at least 58 x 68-inches

A rotary cutter, mat, and wide clear plastic
ruler with 1/8-inch markings are necessary
tools in attaining accuracy.

A 6 x 24-inch ruler is recommended

Jiffy Quilt Top

NOTE: *The yardage given allows for the strips to be cut on the crosswise grain. Diagonally piece the strips as needed, referring to **Diagonal Piecing** on page 67.*

Jiffy Cutting for Quilt Top

From **BLUE DOT:**
- Cut 3, 6-1/2 x 42-inch side border strips
- Cut 3, 6-1/2 x 42-inch strips.
  From the strips cut:
  5, 6-1/2 x 20-1/2-inch rectangles

From **YELLOW PRINT:**
- Cut 3, 6-1/2 x 42-inch strips
- Cut 2, 6-1/2 x 42-inch strips.
  From the strips cut:
  4, 6-1/2 x 20-1/2-inch rectangles

From **BLUE PRINT:**
- Cut 6, 4-1/2 x 42-inch strips

Jiffy Piecing

Step 1   Referring to the Step 2 diagram for placement, align long raw edges and sew together the 5, 6-1/2 x 20-1/2-inch **BLUE DOT** and the 4, 6-1/2 x 20-1/2-inch **YELLOW** rectangles; press. <u>At this point the quilt center should measure 20-1/2 x 54-1/2-inches.</u>

Step 2   For the side borders, measure the quilt from top to bottom through the middle (our quilt is 54-1/2-inches long). With pins, mark the center points along the 2 side edges of the quilt center.

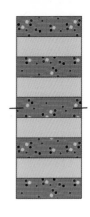

Step 3   Referring to the Step 4 diagram, measure and mark the border lengths and center points on the 4-1/2-inch wide **BLUE PRINT** strips cut for the side borders before sewing them on.

Step 4   Pin the **BLUE PRINT** border strips to the side edges of the quilt center matching the pinned points on each of the borders and the quilt. Stitch a 1/4-inch seam. Press the seam allowances toward the borders. Trim off excess border lengths.

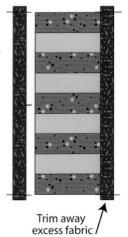

Trim away excess fabric

Step 5   Cut 2 of the 6-1/2-inch wide **YELLOW** strips to the measurement taken in Step 2. Pin and sew the border strips to the side edges of the quilt; press.

Step 6 Cut 2 of the 6-1/2-inch wide **BLUE DOT** strips to the measurement taken in Step 2. Pin and sew the border strips to the side edges of the quilt; press. At this point the center unit should measure 52-1/2 x 54-1/2-inches.

Step 7 For the top/bottom borders, measure the quilt from left to right through the middle, including the seam allowances (our quilt is 52-1/2-inches wide). With pins, mark the center points along the top/bottom edges of the quilt center.

Step 8 Measure and mark the border lengths and center point on the 4-1/2-inch wide **BLUE PRINT** strips cut for the top/bottom borders before sewing them on. Pin the **BLUE PRINT** border strips to the top/bottom edges of the quilt center. At this point the quilt should measure 52-1/2 x 62-1/2-inches.

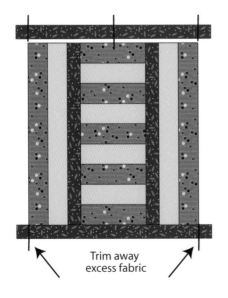

Trim away excess fabric

Putting It All Together

Step 1 Cut the 3-1/4 yard length of backing fabric in half crosswise to make 2, 1-5/8 yard lengths. Sew the long edges together; press. Trim the batting and backing so they are 3-inches larger on all sides than the quilt top.

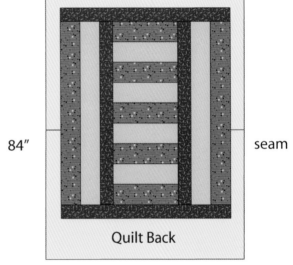

58"

84"

seam

Quilt Back

Finished Back Diagram

Step 2 Mark the quilt top for quilting. Layer the backing, batting, and quilt top. To secure the layers together for hand quilting, use long basting stitches by hand to hold the layers together. Quilt as desired.

Jiffy Quilting Suggestions:

- The **YELLOW** strips - use TB25 Connecting Maze stencil.

- The **BLUE PRINT** strips - meander.

- The **BLUE DOT** strips - quilt with a 1-1/2-inch wide crosshatch design.

*The **THIMBLEBERRIES®** quilt stencils are by Quilting Creations International. To view the quilt stencil designs, see below right.*

Step 3 When quilting is complete, hand baste the 3 layers together a scant 1/4-inch from the edge. This basting keeps the layers from shifting and prevents puckers from forming when adding the binding. Trim excess batting and backing fabric even with the edge of the quilt top.

Jiffy Binding

NOTE: *Refer to* **Binding** *on page 67 for complete binding instructions with detailed illustrations.*

Jiffy Cutting for Binding

From **RED PRINT**:

- Cut 6, 2-3/4 x 42-inch strips

Attaching the Binding

Step 1 Diagonally piece the strips together. Fold the strip in half lengthwise, wrong sides together; press.

Stitch diagonally   Trim to 1/4" seam allowance   Press seam open

Diagonal Piecing

Step 2 With raw edges of the binding and quilt top even, stitch with a 3/8-inch seam allowance.

Step 3 Miter binding at the corners. To do so, stop sewing 3/8-inch from the corner of the quilt. Flip the binding strip up and away from the quilt, then fold the binding down even with the raw edge of the quilt. Begin sewing at the upper edge. Miter all 4 corners in this manner.

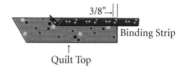

3/8" →
Binding Strip
↑
Quilt Top

Step 4 Bring the folded edge of the binding to the back of the quilt and hand sew the binding in place.

Blueberry Blue
Quilting Suggestion

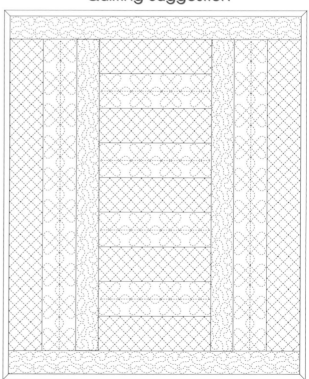

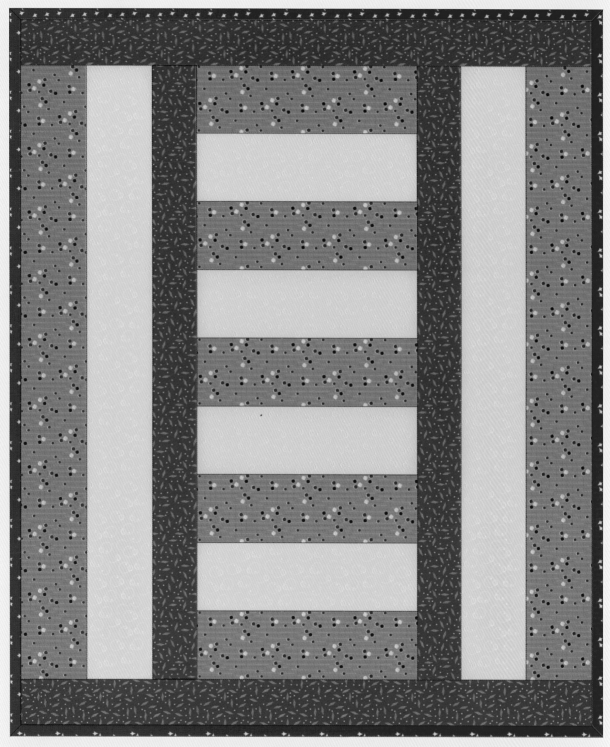

Blueberry Blue
52 x 62-inches

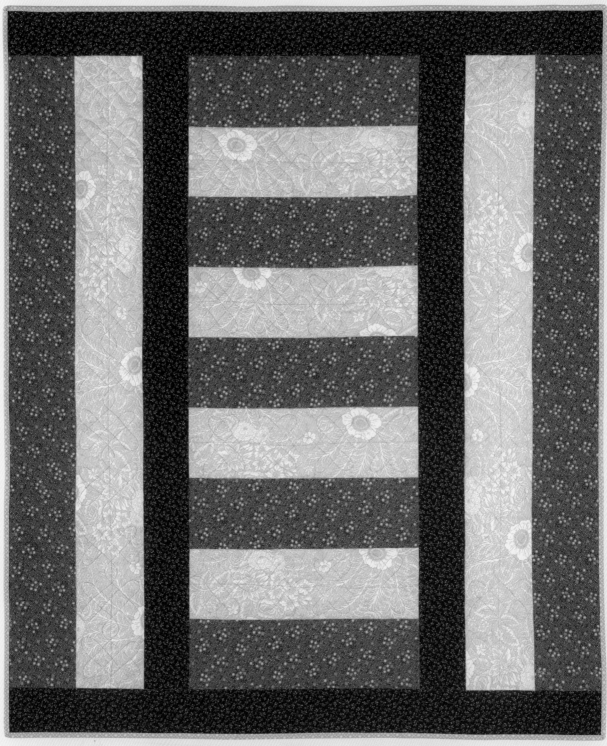

Blueberry Blue—Summer
52 x 62-inches

Blueberry Blue—Autumn
52 x 62-inches

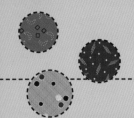
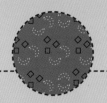

Buttermint Patches

48 x 56-inches

Materials

1-1/4 yards **GREEN DOT**
for quilt center and outer border

2/3 yard **ROSE PRINT**
for quilt center and middle border

1/2 yard **BLUE PRINT** for quilt center

1/3 yard **YELLOW PRINT** for quilt center

5/8 yard **GREEN FLORAL** for inner border

5/8 yard **ROSE PRINT** for binding

3 yards **NAVY/GREEN DIAGONAL PRINT**
for backing

quilt batting, at least 54 x 62-inches

A rotary cutter, mat, and wide clear
plastic ruler with 1/8-inch markings are
necessary tools in attaining accuracy.

A 6 x 24-inch ruler is recommended

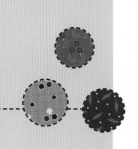

Jiffy Quilt Center

Jiffy Cutting for Quilt Center

From **GREEN DOT**:

- Cut 1, 8-1/2 x 42-inch strip.
  From the strip cut:
    1, 8-1/2-inch center square
    4, 4-1/2-inch squares

From **ROSE PRINT**:

- Cut 1, 4-1/2 x 42-inch strip.
  From the strip cut:
    4, 4-1/2-inch squares
- Cut 1, 2-1/2 x 42-inch strip.
  From the strip cut:
    2, 2-1/2 x 12-1/2-inch strips
    2, 2-1/2 x 8-1/2-inch strips

From **BLUE PRINT**:

- Cut 3, 4-1/2 x 42-inch strips.
  From the strips cut:
    2, 4-1/2 x 20-1/2-inch strips
    2, 4-1/2 x 12-1/2-inch strips
    4, 4-1/2-inch squares

From **YELLOW PRINT**:

- Cut 3, 2-1/2 x 42-inch strips.
  From the strips cut:
    2, 2-1/2 x 24-1/2-inch strips
    2, 2-1/2 x 20-1/2-inch strips

Jiffy Piecing

Step 1   Referring to the quilt center diagram, sew the 2-1/2 x 8-1/2-inch **ROSE** strips to the top/bottom edges of the 8-1/2-inch **GREEN DOT** center square; press. Sew the 2-1/2 x 12-1/2-inch **ROSE** strips to the side edges of the square; press.

Step 2   Sew the 4-1/2 x 12-1/2-inch **BLUE** strips to the top/bottom edges of the center square; press. Sew the 4-1/2 x 20-1/2-inch **BLUE** strips to the side edges of the center square; press. <u>At this point the quilt center should measure 20-1/2-inches square.</u>

Step 3   Sew the 2-1/2 x 20-1/2-inch **YELLOW** strips to the top/bottom edges of the quilt center square; press. Sew the 2-1/2 x 24-1/2-inch **YELLOW** strips to the side edges of the quilt center square; press. <u>At this point the quilt center should measure 24-1/2-inches square.</u>

Step 4   Referring to the diagram for block placement, sew together 2 of each of the **BLUE**, **ROSE**, and **GREEN DOT** 4-1/2-inch squares; press. Make 2 block rows. <u>At this point each block row should measure 4-1/2 x 24-1/2-inches.</u>

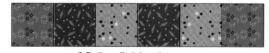

Make 2 block rows

Step 5 Referring to the quilt center diagram for placement, sew the block rows to the top/bottom edges of the quilt center; press. <u>At this point the quilt center should measure 24-1/2 x 32-1/2-inches.</u>

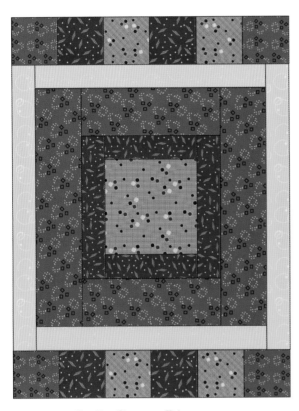

Quilt Center Diagram

Jiffy Borders

NOTE: *The yardage given allows for the border strips to be cut on the crosswise grain. Diagonally piece the strips as needed, referring to* **Diagonal Piecing** *on page 67.*

Jiffy Cutting for Border

From **GREEN FLORAL**:
- Cut 4, 4-1/2 x 42-inch inner border strips

From **ROSE PRINT**:
- Cut 5, 2-1/2 x 42-inch middle border strips

From **GREEN DOT**:
- Cut 5, 6-1/2 x 42-inch outer border strips

Attaching the Borders

Step 1 With pins, mark the center points along all 4 sides of the quilt. For the top/bottom borders, measure the quilt from left to right through the middle. This measurement will give you the most accurate measurement that will result in a "square" quilt.

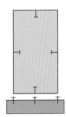

Step 2 Measure and mark the border lengths and center points on the 4-1/2-inch wide **GREEN FLORAL** strips cut for the borders before sewing them on.

Step 3 Pin the border strips to the quilt matching the pinned points on each of the borders and the quilt. Stitch a 1/4-inch seam. Press the seam allowance toward the borders. Trim off excess border lengths.

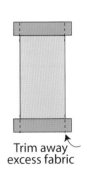

Trim away excess fabric

Step 4   For the side borders, measure your quilt from top to bottom, including the borders just added, to determine the length of the side borders.

Step 5   Measure and mark the 4-1/2-inch wide **GREEN FLORAL** side border lengths as you did for the top/bottom borders.

Step 6   Pin and stitch the side border strips in place; press and trim.

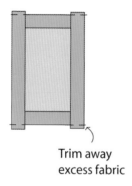

Trim away
excess fabric

Step 7   Repeat Steps 1 through 6 to sew the 2-1/2-inch wide **ROSE** middle border strips to the quilt center and the 6-1/2-inch wide **GREEN DOT** outer border strips to the quilt center; press.

Putting It All Together

Step 1   Cut the 3 yard length of backing fabric in half crosswise to make 2, 1-1/2 yard lengths. Sew the long edges together; press. Trim the batting and backing so they are 3-inches larger on all sides than the quilt top.

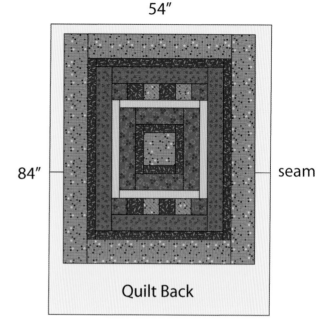

Finished Back Diagram

Step 2   Mark the quilt top for quilting. Layer the backing, batting, and quilt top. To secure the layers together for hand quilting, use long basting stitches by hand to hold the layers together. Quilt as desired.

Jiffy Quilting Suggestions:

• The **GREEN** center square
  - use TB8 Water Lily stencil.

• The **BLUE** and **GREEN FLORAL** borders - use TB31 Blossom Swirl stencil.

• The **YELLOW** border
  - use TB30 Beadwork stencil.

• The **ROSE** borders - meander.

• The block rows - quilt an X in each square.

• The **GREEN DOT** outer border - quilt with a 1-1/2-inch crosshatch design.

*The **THIMBLEBERRIES**® quilt stencils are by Quilting Creations International. To view the quilt stencil designs, refer to page 102.*

Step 3 When quilting is complete, hand baste the 3 layers together a scant 1/4-inch from the edge. This basting keeps the layers from shifting and prevents puckers from forming when adding the binding. Trim excess batting and backing fabric even with the edge of the quilt top.

Jiffy Binding

NOTE: *Refer to **Binding** on page 67 for complete binding instructions with detailed illustrations.*

Jiffy Cutting for Binding

From **ROSE PRINT**:

- Cut 6, 2-3/4 x 42-inch strips

Attaching the Binding

Step 1 Diagonally piece the strips together. Fold the strip in half lengthwise, wrong sides together; press.

Stitch diagonally   Trim to 1/4" seam allowance   Press seam open

Diagonal Piecing

Step 2 With raw edges of the binding and quilt top even, stitch with a 3/8-inch seam allowance.

Step 3 Miter binding at the corners. To do so, stop sewing 3/8-inch from the corner of the quilt. Flip the binding strip up and away from the quilt, then fold the binding down even with the raw edge of the quilt. Begin sewing at the upper edge. Miter all 4 corners in this manner.

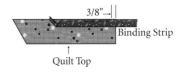

3/8"→

Binding Strip

Quilt Top

Step 4 Bring the folded edge of the binding to the back of the quilt and hand sew the binding in place.

Buttermint Patches
Quilting Suggestion

Buttermint Patches
48 x 56-inches

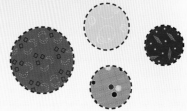

Buttermint Patches—Floral Center
48 x 56-inches

Buttermint Patches—Green Center

48 x 56-inches

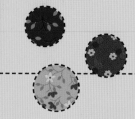
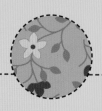

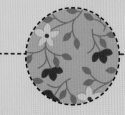

Pinwheel Twist

48 x 64-inches

Materials

1 yard **RED PRINT**
for pinwheel blocks and inner border

1/2 yard **TAN PRINT** for pinwheel blocks

3/4 yard **BLACK PRINT**
for pinwheel blocks and lattice post squares

7/8 yard **BEIGE PRINT** for lattice segments

1 yard **GREEN PRINT** for outer border

1/2 yard **RED PRINT** for binding

3 yards **TAN PRINT** for backing

quilt batting, at least 54 x 70-inches

A rotary cutter, mat, and wide clear plastic
ruler with 1/8-inch markings are necessary
tools in attaining accuracy.

A 6 x 24-inch ruler is recommended

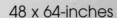

Jiffy Quilt Center

Makes 6 blocks

Jiffy Cutting for Pinwheel Blocks

From **RED PRINT**:
- Cut 3, 6-7/8 x 42-inch strips.
  From the strips cut:
  12, 6-7/8-inch squares.
  Cut the squares in half
  diagonally to make 24 triangles.

From **TAN PRINT**:
- Cut 2, 7-1/4 x 42-inch strips.
  From the strips cut:
  6, 7-1/4-inch squares

From **BLACK PRINT**:
- Cut 2, 7-1/4 x 42-inch strips.
  From the strips cut:
  6, 7-1/4-inch squares

Jiffy Piecing

Step 1 With right sides together, layer
the 7-1/4-inch **TAN** and **BLACK**
squares in pairs. Press together,
but do not sew. Cut the layered
squares diagonally into quarters
to make 24 sets of triangles.
Stitch along the same bias edge
of each pair of triangles being
careful not to stretch the
triangles; press.

*(**TAN** fabric is under **BLACK**)*

Bias edges

Make 24 triangle units

Step 2 Sew the **RED** triangles to the
edge of each triangle unit; press.
At this point each pieced square
should measure 6-1/2-inches
square. Sew the pieced squares
together in pairs; press. Sew
the pairs together to make
the pinwheel blocks; press.
At this point each pinwheel
block should measure
12-1/2-inches square.

Make 24   *Make 12*

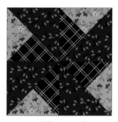

Make 6

Jiffy Quilt Center

Jiffy Cutting for the Quilt Center

From **BLACK PRINT**:
- Cut 2, 4-1/2 x 42-inch strips.
  From the strips cut:
  12, 4-1/2-inch lattice
  post squares

From **BEIGE PRINT**:
- Cut 6, 4-1/2 x 42-inch strips.
  From the strips cut:
  17, 4-1/2 x 12-1/2-inch
  lattice segments

Quilt Center Assembly

Step 1   Referring to the diagram for block placement, sew together 3 of the 4-1/2 x 12-1/2-inch **BEIGE** lattice segments and 2 of the pinwheel blocks. Press the seam allowances toward the lattice segments. <u>At this point each block row should measure 12-1/2 x 36-1/2-inches.</u>

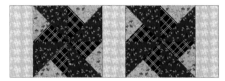

Make 3 block rows

Step 2   Sew together 2 of the 4-1/2 x 12-1/2-inch **BEIGE** lattice segments and 3 of the 4-1/2-inch **BLACK** lattice post squares. Press the seam allowances toward the lattice segments. <u>At this point each lattice strip should measure 4-1/2 x 36-1/2-inches.</u>

Make 4 lattice strips

Step 3   Referring to the quilt diagram, sew together the block rows and lattice strips; press. <u>At this point the quilt center should measure 36-1/2 x 52-1/2-inches.</u>

Jiffy Borders

NOTE*: The yardage given allows for the border strips to be cut on the crosswise grain. Diagonally piece the strips as needed, referring to **Diagonal Piecing** on page 67.*

Jiffy Cutting for Borders

From **RED PRINT**:
- Cut 5, 2 x 42-inch inner border strips

From **GREEN PRINT**:
- Cut 6, 5 x 42-inch outer border strips

Attaching the Borders

Step 1   With pins, mark the center points along all 4 sides of the quilt. For the top/bottom borders, measure the quilt from left to right through the middle. This measurement will give you the most accurate measurement that will result in a "square" quilt.

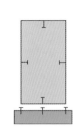

Step 2   Measure and mark the border lengths and center points on the 2-inch wide **RED** strips cut for the borders before sewing them on.

Step 3   Pin the border strips to the quilt matching the pinned points on each of the borders and the quilt. Stitch a 1/4-inch seam. Press the seam allowance toward the borders. Trim off excess border lengths.

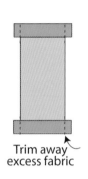

Trim away excess fabric

Step 4   For the side borders, measure your quilt from top to bottom, including the borders just added, to determine the length of the side borders.

Step 5   Measure and mark the 2-inch wide **RED** side border lengths as you did for the top/bottom borders.

Step 6   Pin and stitch the side border strips in place; press and trim.

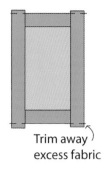

Trim away excess fabric

Step 7   Attach the 5-inch wide **GREEN** outer border strips in the same manner.

Putting It All Together

Step 1   Cut the 3 yard length of backing fabric in half crosswise to make 2, 1-1/2 yard lengths. Sew the long edges together; press. Trim the batting and backing so they are 3-inches larger on all sides than the quilt top.

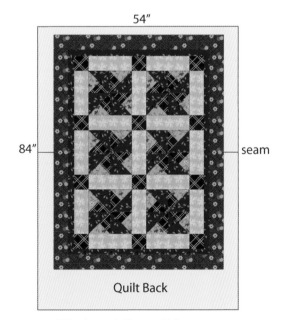

54"

84"   seam

Quilt Back

Finished Back Diagram

Step 2 Mark the quilt top for quilting. Layer the backing, batting, and quilt top. To secure the layers together for hand quilting, use long basting stitches by hand to hold the layers together. Quilt as desired.

Jiffy Quilting Suggestions:

- The pinwheel blocks - use TB8 Leaf Quartet stencil.
- The **BLACK** lattice post squares - use TB23 Flower Burst stencil.
- The **GREEN** outer border - use TB37 Pansy Vine stencil.
- The **BEIGE** lattice segments - channel stitch.
- The **RED** inner border - meander.

*The **THIMBLEBERRIES**® quilt stencils are by Quilting Creations International. To view the quilt stencil designs, refer to page 112.*

Step 3 When quilting is complete, hand baste the 3 layers together a scant 1/4-inch from the edge. This basting keeps the layers from shifting and prevents puckers from forming when adding the binding. Trim excess batting and backing fabric even with the edge of the quilt top.

Jiffy Binding

NOTE: *Refer to **Binding** on page 67 for complete binding instructions with detailed illustrations.*

Jiffy Cutting for Binding

From **RED PRINT**:
- Cut 6, 2-3/4 x 42-inch strips

Attaching the Binding

Step 1 Diagonally piece the strips together. Fold the strip in half lengthwise, wrong sides together; press.

Stitch diagonally   Trim to 1/4" seam allowance   Press seam open

Diagonal Piecing

Step 2 With raw edges of the binding and quilt top even, stitch with a 3/8-inch seam allowance.

Step 3 Miter binding at the corners. To do so, stop sewing 3/8-inch from the corner of the quilt. Flip the binding strip up and away from the quilt, then fold the binding down even with the raw edge of the quilt. Begin sewing at the upper edge. Miter all 4 corners in this manner.

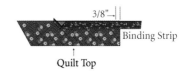

3/8" Binding Strip
Quilt Top

Step 4 Bring the folded edge of the binding to the back of the quilt and hand sew the binding in place.

Pinwheel Twist

Quilting Suggestion

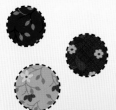

Pinwheel Twist

48 x 64-inches

Pinwheel Twist—Spring

48 x 64-inches

Pinwheel Twist—Christmas

48 x 64-inches

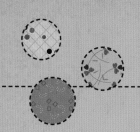
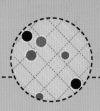

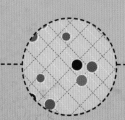
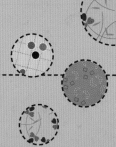

Rainbow Sherbet

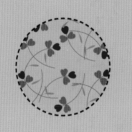

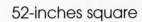

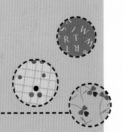

52-inches square

Materials

5/8 yard **BLUE ALPHABET PRINT**
for hourglass blocks

1-1/8 yards **BEIGE PRINT** for hourglass blocks

3/4 yard **YELLOW DOT**
for hourglass blocks and corner squares

1/2 yard **ROSE FLORAL** for border

1/2 yard **GREEN PRINT** for border

5/8 yard **BLUE ALPHABET PRINT** for binding

3-1/4 yards **GREEN DOT** for backing

quilt batting, at least 58-inches square

A rotary cutter, mat, and wide clear plastic
ruler with 1/8-inch markings are necessary
tools in attaining accuracy.

A 6 x 24-inch ruler is recommended

Jiffy Quilt Center

***Makes 15** BLUE/BEIGE blocks*

***Makes 10** YELLOW/BEIGE blocks*

Jiffy Cutting for Hourglass Blocks

From **BLUE ALPHABET PRINT**:

- Cut 2, 9-1/4 x 42-inch strips.
  From the strips cut:
  8, 9-1/4-inch squares

From **BEIGE PRINT**:

- Cut 4, 9-1/4 x 42-inch strips.
  From the strips cut:
  13, 9-1/4-inch squares

From **YELLOW DOT**:

- Cut 2, 9-1/4 x 42-inch strips.
  From the strips cut:
  5, 9-1/4-inch squares

Jiffy Piecing

Step 1 With right sides together, layer the 9-1/4-inch **BLUE ALPHABET PRINT** squares and 8 of the 9-1/4-inch **BEIGE** squares in pairs. Press together, but do not sew. Cut the layered squares diagonally into quarters to make 30 sets of triangles. (You will have extra triangle sets.) Stitch along the same bias edge of each pair of triangles being careful not to stretch the triangles; press. Sew the triangle units together in pairs; press.

At this point each hourglass block should measure 8-1/2-inches square.

*(**BLUE** fabric is under **BEIGE**)*

Bias edges

Make 30 triangle units   *Make 15 hourglass blocks*

Step 2 With right sides together, layer the 9-1/4-inch **YELLOW DOT** squares and 5 of the 9-1/4-inch **BEIGE** squares in pairs. Press together, but do not sew. Cut the layered squares diagonally into quarters to make 20 sets of triangles. Stitch along the same bias edge of each pair of triangles being careful not to stretch the triangles; press. Sew the triangle units together in pairs; press. At this point each hourglass block should measure 8-1/2-inches square.

*(**YELLOW** fabric is under **BEIGE**)*

Bias edges

Make 20 triangle units   *Make 10 hourglass blocks*

Step 3 Referring to the block row diagrams for block placement, lay out the hourglass blocks in 5 rows with 5 blocks each.

Sew the blocks together in each row. <u>At this point each block row should measure 8-1/2 x 40-1/2-inches.</u> Press the seam allowances in alternating directions by rows so the seams will fit snugly together with less bulk.

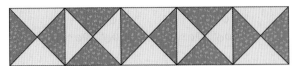

Make 3 block rows

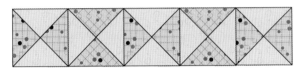

Make 2 block rows

Step 4 Referring to the quilt center diagram for placement, pin the block rows together at the block intersections; sew and press. <u>At this point the quilt center should measure 40-1/2-inches square.</u>

Jiffy Border

NOTE: *The yardage given allows for the border strips to be cut on the crosswise grain.*

Jiffy Cutting for Borders

From **ROSE FLORAL**:
- Cut 2, 6-1/2 x 42-inch border strips

From **GREEN PRINT**:
- Cut 2, 6-1/2 x 42-inch border strips

From **YELLOW DOT**:
- Cut 1, 6-1/2 x 42-inch strip.
  From the strip cut:
  4, 6-1/2-inch corner squares

Attaching the Border

Step 1 With pins, mark the center points along all 4 sides of the quilt. For the top/bottom borders, measure the quilt from left to right through the middle. This measurement will give you the most accurate measurement that will result in a "square" quilt.

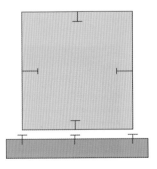

Step 2 Measure and mark the border lengths and center point on the 6-1/2-inch wide **ROSE FLORAL** strips cut for the borders before sewing them on.

Step 3 Pin the border strips to the quilt matching the pinned points on each of the borders and the quilt. Stitch a 1/4-inch seam. Press the seam allowance toward the borders. Trim off excess border lengths.

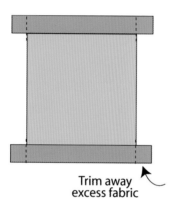

Trim away
excess fabric

Step 4 For the side borders, measure the quilt from top to bottom through the middle including the seam allowances, but not the borders just added. Cut the 2, 6-1/2-inch wide **GREEN** strips to this length. Sew 6-1/2-inch **YELLOW DOT** corner squares to both ends of the **GREEN** side border strips; press. Sew the borders to the side edges of the quilt; press.

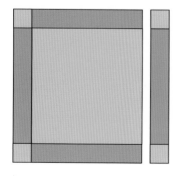

Putting It All Together

Step 1 Cut the 3-1/4 yard length of backing fabric in half crosswise to make 2, 1-5/8 yard lengths. Sew the long edges together; press. Trim the batting and backing so they are 3-inches larger on all sides than the quilt top.

58"

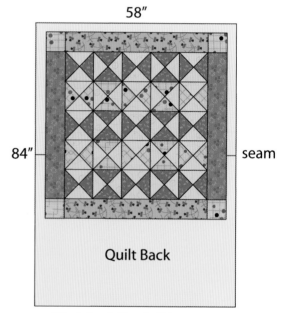

84"   seam

Quilt Back

Finished Back Diagram

Step 2 Mark the quilt top for quilting. Layer the backing, batting, and quilt top. To secure the layers together for hand quilting, use long basting stitches by hand to hold the layers together. Quilt as desired.

Jiffy Quilting Suggestions:

• The **BLUE ALPHABET PRINT** hourglass blocks - use TB5 Wings stencil.

• The **YELLOW DOT** hourglass blocks - use TB20 Tulips stencil.

- The **YELLOW DOT** corner squares - use TB23 Flower Burst stencil.

- The border strips - use TB36 Flutter Bug stencil.

*The **THIMBLEBERRIES**® quilt stencils are by Quilting Creations International. To view the quilt stencil designs, refer to page 122.*

Step 3 When quilting is complete, hand baste the 3 layers together a scant 1/4-inch from the edge. This basting keeps the layers from shifting and prevents puckers from forming when adding the binding. Trim excess batting and backing fabric even with the edge of the quilt top.

Jiffy Binding

NOTE: *Refer to **Binding** on page 67 for complete binding instructions with detailed illustrations.*

Jiffy Cutting for Binding

From **BLUE ALPHABET PRINT**:

- Cut 6, 2-3/4 x 42-inch strips

Attaching the Binding

Step 1 Diagonally piece the strips together. Fold the strip in half lengthwise, wrong sides together; press.

Stitch diagonally   Trim to 1/4" seam allowance   Press seam open

Diagonal Piecing

Step 2 With raw edges of the binding and quilt top even, stitch with a 3/8-inch seam allowance.

Step 3 Miter binding at the corners. To do so, stop sewing 3/8-inch from the corner of the quilt. Flip the binding strip up and away from the quilt, then fold the binding down even with the raw edge of the quilt. Begin sewing at the upper edge. Miter all 4 corners in this manner.

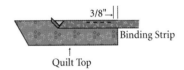

Step 4 Bring the folded edge of the binding to the back of the quilt and hand sew the binding in place.

Rainbow Sherbet

Quilting Suggestion

Rainbow Sherbet
52-inches square

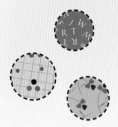

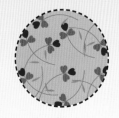

Rainbow Sherbet—Parade

52-inches square

Rainbow Sherbet—Autumn

52-inches square

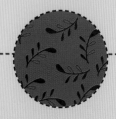
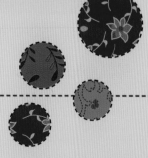

Spice is Nice

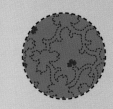

48 x 54-inches

Materials

1/2 yard **RUSSET PRINT**
for triangle-pieced square blocks

1/2 yard **BEIGE PRINT**
for triangle-pieced square blocks

1/2 yard **GREEN PRINT**
for lattice strips and inner border

5/8 yard **GOLD PRINT** for middle border

1 yard **BRICK FLORAL** for outer border

1/2 yard **GREEN PRINT** for binding

3 yards **TAN PRINT** for backing

quilt batting, at least 54 x 60-inches

A rotary cutter, mat, and wide clear
plastic ruler with 1/8-inch markings are
necessary tools in attaining accuracy.

A 6 x 24-inch ruler is recommended

Jiffy Quilt Center

Makes 16 blocks

Jiffy Cutting for Triangle-Pieced Squares

From **RUSSET PRINT:**

* Cut 2, 6-7/8 x 42-inch strips

From **BEIGE PRINT:**

* Cut 2, 6-7/8 x 42-inch strips

Jiffy Piecing

Step 1   With right sides together, layer the 6-7/8 x 42-inch **RUSSET** and **BEIGE** strips in pairs. Press together, but do not sew. Cut the layered strips into squares. Cut the layered squares in half diagonally to make 16 sets of triangles. Stitch 1/4-inch from the diagonal edge of each pair of triangles; press.

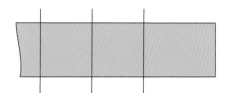

Crosscut 8, 6-7/8-inch squares
(RUSSET *fabric is under* **BEIGE)**

(RUSSET *fabric is under* **BEIGE)**

Make 16, 6-1/2-inch triangle-pieced squares

Step 2   Sew 4 of the triangle-pieced squares together in a row; press. Noting the direction of

seam lines, make a total of 4 block rows. <u>At this point each block row should measure 6-1/2 x 24-1/2-inches.</u>

Jiffy Quilt Center

Jiffy Cutting for Quilt Center

From **GREEN PRINT:**

* Cut 4, 2-1/2 x 42-inch strips. Diagonally piece the strips as needed. From the strips cut: 5, 2-1/2 x 24-1/2-inch top/bottom inner border/lattice strips (or the length of the block rows)

Referring to the quilt diagram for block placement, sew together the block rows and the 5, 2-1/2 x 24-1/2-inch **GREEN** top/bottom inner border/lattice strips; press. <u>At this point the quilt center should measure 24-1/2 x 34-1/2-inches.</u>

Jiffy Border

NOTE: *The yardage given allows for the border strips to be cut on the crosswise grain. Diagonally piece the strips as needed, referring to **Diagonal Piecing** on page 67.*

Jiffy Cutting for Border

From **GREEN PRINT:**
- Cut 2, 2-1/2 x 42-inch side inner border strips

From **GOLD PRINT:**
- Cut 4, 4-1/2 x 42-inch middle border strips

From **BRICK FLORAL:**
- Cut 5, 6-1/2 x 42-inch outer border strips

Attaching the Borders

Step 1   With pins, mark the center points along all 4 sides of the quilt. For the side inner borders, measure your quilt from top to bottom, including the borders just added, to determine the length of the side borders. This measurement will give you the most accurate measurement that will result in a "square" quilt.

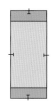

Step 2   Measure and mark the 2-1/2-inch wide **GREEN** side border lengths.

Step 3   Pin and stitch the side border strips in place; press and trim.

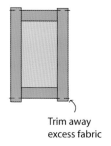

Trim away
excess fabric

Step 4   For the top/bottom middle borders, measure the quilt from left to right through the middle.

Step 5   Measure and mark the border lengths and center points on the 4-1/2-inch wide **GOLD** strips cut for the borders before sewing them on.

Step 6   Pin the border strips to the quilt matching the pinned points on each of the borders and the quilt. Stitch a 1/4-inch seam. Press the seam allowance toward the borders. Trim off excess border lengths.

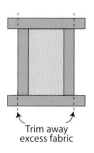

Trim away
excess fabric

Step 7   Attach the 4-1/2-inch wide **GOLD** middle side border strips and the 6-1/2-inch wide **BRICK FLORAL** outer border strips in the same manner.

Putting It All Together

The **THIMBLEBERRIES®** quilt stencils are by Quilting Creations International. To view the quilt stencil designs, refer to page 132.

Step 1 Cut the 3 yard length of backing fabric in half crosswise to make 2, 1-1/2 yard lengths. Sew the long edges together; press. Trim the batting and backing so they are 3-inches larger on all sides than the quilt top.

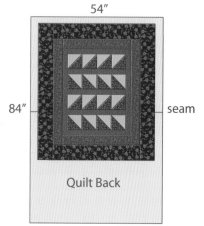

Finished Back Diagram

Step 2 Mark the quilt top for quilting. Layer the backing, batting, and quilt top. To secure the layers together for hand quilting, use long basting stitches by hand to hold the layers together. Quilt as desired.

Jiffy Quilting Suggestions:

- The triangle-pieced square blocks - use TB17 Lady Slipper stencil.

- The **GREEN** lattice/inner border - use TB30 Beadwork stencil.

- The **GOLD** middle border - use TB35 Flutter Bug stencil.

- The **BRICK FLORAL** outer border - use TB32 Blossom Swirl stencil.

Step 3 When quilting is complete, hand baste the 3 layers together a scant 1/4-inch from the edge. This basting keeps the layers from shifting and prevents puckers from forming when adding the binding. Trim excess batting and backing fabric even with the edge of the quilt top.

Jiffy Binding

NOTE: *Refer to **Binding** on page 67 for complete binding instructions with detailed illustrations.*

Jiffy Cutting for Binding

From **GREEN PRINT:**

- Cut 6, 2-3/4 x 42-inch strips

Attaching the Binding

Step 1 Diagonally piece the strips together. Fold the strip in half lengthwise, wrong sides together; press.

Stitch diagonally   Trim to 1/4" seam allowance   Press seam open

Diagonal Piecing

Step 2   With raw edges of the binding and quilt top even, stitch with a 3/8-inch seam allowance.

Step 3   Miter binding at the corners. To do so, stop sewing 3/8-inch from the corner of the quilt. Flip the binding strip up and away from the quilt, then fold the binding down even with the raw edge of the quilt. Begin sewing at the upper edge. Miter all 4 corners in this manner.

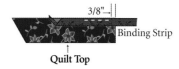

3/8"

Binding Strip

Quilt Top

Step 4   Bring the folded edge of the binding to the back of the quilt and hand sew the binding in place.

Spice is Nice

Quilting Suggestion

Spice is Nice
48 x 54-inches

Spice is Nice—Dot Border

48 x 54-inches

Spice is Nice—Roses Border

48 x 54-inches

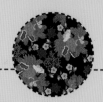

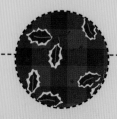

Checkerboard Runner

18 x 40-inches

Materials

1/3 yard **RED PRINT**
for checkerboard section and middle border

1/3 yard **BEIGE PRINT**
for checkerboard section

1/4 yard **LARGE BLACK FLORAL**
for inner border

1/8 yard **GOLD PRINT** for middle border

1/4 yard **GREEN DIAGONAL CHECK**
for outer border

3/8 yard **GOLD PRINT** for binding

1-1/4 yards for backing

quilt batting, at least 24 x 46-inches

A rotary cutter, mat, and wide clear
plastic ruler with 1/8-inch markings are
necessary tools in attaining accuracy.

A 6 x 24-inch ruler is recommended

Checkerboard Section

Jiffy Cutting

From **RED PRINT:**
- Cut 3, 2-1/2 x 42-inch strips

From **BEIGE PRINT:**
- Cut 3, 2-1/2 x 42-inch strips

Jiffy Piecing

Step 1 Aligning long edges, sew 2-1/2 x 42-inch **RED** strips to the top/bottom edges of a 2-1/2 x 42-inch **BEIGE** strip. Press the seam allowances toward the **RED** strips. Make 1 strip set. Cut the strip set into segments.

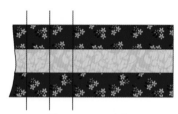

Crosscut 11,
2-1/2-inch wide segments

Step 2 Aligning long edges, sew 2-1/2 x 42-inch **BEIGE** strips to the top/bottom edges of a 2-1/2 x 42-inch **RED** strip. Press the seam allowances toward the **RED** strip. Make 1 strip set. Cut the strip set into segments.

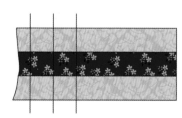

Crosscut 10,
2-1/2-inch wide segments

Step 3 Referring to the diagrams, sew together the segments in 3 units; press. Each unit should measure 6-1/2 x 14-1/2-inches. Referring to the runner diagram, sew the units together to make the checkerboard section; press. At this point the checkerboard section should measure 14-1/2 x 18-1/2-inches.

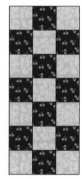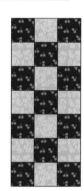

| *Make 1* | *Make 1* | *Make 1* |

Jiffy Borders

NOTE: *The yardage given allows for the border strips to be cut on the crosswise grain. Read through* **Border** *instructions on page 39 for general instructions on adding borders.*

Jiffy Cutting

From **LARGE BLACK FLORAL:**
- Cut 2, 6-1/2 x 18-1/2-inch inner border strips

From **GOLD PRINT:**
- Cut 2, 1-1/2 x 18-1/2-inch middle border strips

From **RED PRINT:**
- Cut 2, 2-1/2 x 18-1/2-inch middle border strips

From **GREEN DIAGONAL CHECK:**
- Cut 2, 4-1/2 x 18-1/2-inch outer border strips

Attaching the Borders

Step 1   Attach the 6-1/2-inch wide **LARGE BLACK FLORAL** inner border strips.

Step 2   Attach the 1-1/2-inch wide **GOLD** middle border strips.

Step 3   Attach the 2-1/2-inch wide **RED** middle border strips.

Step 4   Attach the 4-1/2-inch wide **GREEN DIAGONAL CHECK** outer border strips.

Putting It All Together

*Trim the backing and batting so they are 6-inches larger than the runner top. Refer to **Finishing the Quilt** on page 66 for complete instructions.*

Jiffy Quilting Suggestions:

- The checkerboard section - in-the-ditch.
- The 4 borders - meander.

Jiffy Binding

NOTE: *Refer to **Binding** on page 67 for complete instructions with detailed illustrations.*

Jiffy Cutting for Binding

From **GOLD PRINT:**
- Cut 4, 2-3/4 x 42-inch strips

Attaching the Binding

Step 1   Diagonally piece the strips together. Fold the strip in half lengthwise, wrong sides together; press.

Stitch diagonally   Trim to 1/4" seam allowance   Press seam open

Diagonal Piecing

Step 2   With raw edges of the binding and runner top even, stitch with a 3/8-inch seam allowance.

Step 3   Miter binding at the corners. To do so, stop sewing 3/8-inch from the corner of the runner top. Flip the binding strip up and away from the runner, then fold the binding down even with the raw edge of the runner. Begin sewing at the upper edge. Miter all 4 corners in this manner.

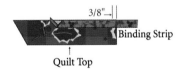

3/8"→|| Binding Strip

Quilt Top

Step 4   Bring the folded edge of the binding to the back of the runner and hand sew the binding in place.

Checkerboard Runner

Quilting Suggestion

Checkerboard Runner
18 x 40-inches

GLOSSARY

Appliqué The sewing technique for attaching pieces (appliqués) of fabric onto a background fabric. Appliqués may be stitched to the background by hand, using a blind stitch, or by machine, using a satin stitch or a blind hemstitch.

Background quilting A quilting style that is used to fill in large, open spaces on a quilt.

Backing The bottom layer of a quilt consisting of one whole piece of fabric or several fabrics joined together.

Basting The technique for joining layers of fabric or the layers of a quilt with safety pins (pin basting) or large stitches (hand basting). The pinning or stitching is temporary and is removed after permanent stitching.

Basting spray Adhesive available in a spray can that may be used to hold the layers of a quilt together instead of hand or pin basting.

Batting A layer of filler placed between two pieces of fabric to form a quilt. Its thickness and fiber content varies.

Bias The grain of woven fabric that is at a 45-degree angle to the selvages. The bias grain has more stretch and is less stable than the crosswise or lengthwise grain.

Bias strips Strips of fabric cut on the bias and joined to make one continuous strip for binding that can easily be positioned around curved edges.

Binding The strip of fabric used to cover the outside edges—top, batting and backing—of a quilt.

Block A basic unit, usually square and often repeated, of a quilt top.

Borders The framing on a quilt that serves to visually hold in the design and give the eye a stopping point.

Channel quilting Parallel rows of straight-line quilting going in one direction across a quilt top.

Color value The lightness or darkness of a fabric's color or hue.

Corner square Square of fabric used to anchor the four corners of a quilt border.

Crosscutting Cutting fabric strips into smaller units, such as squares or rectangles.

Crosswise grain The threads running perpendicular to the selvage across the width of a woven fabric.

Cutting mat Surface used for rotary cutting that protects the tabletop and keeps the fabric from shifting while cutting. Often mats are labeled as self-healing, meaning the blade does not leave slash marks or grooves in the surface even after repeated use.

Design quilting This style of quilting is often achieved by using quilting stencils and marking the quilt top.

Double-fold binding Binding made from a fabric strip that is folded in half before being attached to the quilt. Also, referred to as French-fold binding.

Echo quilting A type of outline quilting in which the first line of quilting is quilted in-the-ditch of an appliqué or other design. The next line is quilted a measurement (i.e., 1/2-inch) away from the first, and subsequent lines 1/2-inch from previous lines, echoing its shape.

Fat Quarter A piece of fabric measuring approximately 18 x 20-inches.

Finished size The measurement of a completed block or quilt.

Flannel A 100% cotton fabric that has a brushed, napped surface.

Free-motion or machine quilting A process of quilting done with the feed dogs disengaged and using a darning presser foot so the quilt can be moved freely on the machine bed in any direction.

GLOSSARY

Grain The direction of woven fabric. The crosswise grain is from selvage to selvage. The lengthwise grain runs parallel to the selvage and is stronger. The bias grain is at a 45-degree angle and has the greatest amount of stretch.

Hand quilting Series of running stitches made through all layers of a quilt with needle and thread.

Hanging Sleeve Tube of fabric that is attached to the quilt back. A wooden dowel is inserted through the fabric tube to hang the quilt. It is also called a rod pocket and used with a board or rod as a support to hang a quilt on the wall.

Inner border A strip of fabric, usually more narrow than the outer border, that frames the quilt center.

In-the-ditch quilting A line of quilting stitches made immediately next to a seam or around an appliqué shape, usually on the side without the seam allowance.

Ironing The process of moving the iron while it has contact with the fabric, which can stretch and distort fabrics and seams. Ironing is distinctly different from pressing.

Lattice post squares Fabric squares or blocks used to separate lattice segments.

Lattice segments Fabric strips used to separate block designs.

Layering Placing the quilt top, batting and quilt backing on top of each other in layers.

Lengthwise grain The threads running parallel to the selvage in a woven fabric.

Loft The thickness of the batting.

Long-arm quilting A quilting machine used by professional quilters in which the quilt is held taut on a frame that allows the quilter to work on a large portion of the quilt at a time. The machine head moves freely, allowing the operator to use free-motion to quilt in all directions.

Machine quilting Series of stitches made through all layers of a quilt sandwich with a sewing machine.

Marking tools A variety of pens, pencils and chalks that can be used to mark fabric pieces or a quilt top.

Meandering quilting An allover quilting pattern characterized by a series of large, loosely curved lines that usually do not cross over one another. Commonly used to cover an entire quilt surface without regard for block or border seams or edges.

Mitered seam A 45-degree angle seam.

On point Quilt blocks that are positioned on the diagonal are on point.

Outer border A strip of fabric that is joined to the edges of the quilt top to finish or frame it.

Outline quilting Stitching that follows the outline of a pieced or appliquéd block by stitching approximately 1/4-inch away from the edge of the shape.

Pieced border Blocks or pieced units sewn together to make a single border unit that is then sewn to the quilt center.

Piecing The process of sewing pieces of fabric together.

Pin baste Process of basting together quilt layers using pins (most often safety pins).

Presser foot The removable machine accessory that holds fabric in place against the machine bed and accommodates the needle. A variety of presser feet styles are available for most machines.

Pressing Using an iron with an up and down motion to set stitches and flatten a seam allowance, rather than sliding it across the fabric.

GLOSSARY

Quilt center The quilt top before borders are added.

Quilt sandwich The three parts of a quilt layered together—the quilt top, batting and backing.

Quilt top Top layer of a quilt usually consisting of pieced blocks.

Quilting The small running stitches made through the layers of a quilt (quilt top, batting and backing) to form decorative patterns on the surface of the quilt and hold the layers together.

Quilting frame/hoop Two pieces of wood or plastic that are placed on the top and bottom of a quilt to hold the fabric taut for quilting.

Quilting stencils Quilting patterns with open areas through which a design is transferred onto a quilt top. May be purchased or made from sturdy, reusable template plastic.

Raw edge The cut end of fabric.

Rotary cutter Tool with a sharp, round blade attached to a handle that is used to cut fabric. The blade is available in different diameters.

Rotary cutting The process of cutting fabric into strips and pieces using a revolving blade rotary cutter, a thick, clear plastic ruler and a special cutting mat.

Running stitches A series of in-and-out stitches used in hand quilting.

Seam allowance The 1/4-inch margin of fabric between the stitched seam and the raw edge.

Selvage The lengthwise finished edge on each side of the fabric.

Slipstitch A hand stitch used for finishing such as sewing binding to a quilt where the thread is hidden by slipping the needle between a fold of fabric and tacking down with small stitches.

Squaring up or straightening fabric The process of trimming the raw edge of the fabric so it creates a 90-degree angle with the folded edge of the fabric. Squaring up is also a term used when trimming a quilt block.

Stipple quilting (also known as tiny meandering) Random curves or designs that flow across the quilt's surface.

Strip sets Two or more strips of fabric, cut and sewn together along the length of the strips.

Thread basting Basting quilt layers together using a needle and thread and extra-long stitches that will be removed after the quilting is complete.

Triangle-pieced square The square unit created when two 90-degree triangles are sewn together on the diagonal.

Tying Taking a stitch through all three layers of the quilt and knotting it on the quilt surface. Tying creates a loftier quilt.

Unfinished size The measurement of a block before the 1/4-inch seam allowance is sewn or the quilt is quilted and bound.

Unit A combination of at least two pieces of fabric sewn together that form part of a block.

Walking foot A sewing machine foot that has grippers on the bottom that act in tandem with the machine's feed dogs to evenly feed multiple layers of fabric and batting beneath the foot. Effective for machine quilting. Also called an even-feed foot.